baby & toddler
Knits
made easy

baby & toddler Knits made easy

LONDON, NEW YORK, MUNICH,
MELBOURNE, DELHI

DK UK
Senior Designer Glenda Fisher
Project Editor Kathryn Meeker
Designers Elaine Hewson and Clare Marshall
Managing Editor Penny Smith
Managing Art Editor Marianne Markham
Senior Jacket Creative Nicola Powling
Assistant Jacket Designer Rosie Levine
Producer, Pre-Production Raymond Williams
Senior Producer Seyhan Esen
Creative Technical Support Sonia Charbonnier
Photography Ruth Jenkinson
Art Direction for Photography Isabel de Cordova
Art Director Jane Bull
Publisher Mary Ling

DK INDIA
Senior Editor Alicia Ingty
Editor Janashree Singha
Senior Art Editor Anchal Kaushal
Art Editors Simran Kaur and Zaurin Thoidingjam
Assistant Art Editor Vikas Sachdeva
Managing Editor Glenda Fernandes
Managing Art Editor Navidita Thapa
Production Manager Pankaj Sharma
CTS Manager Sunil Sharma
DTP Designers Anurag Trivedi, Sachin Singh,
Satish Chandra Gaur, and Syed Md Farhan
Illustrator Subhash Vohra

First published in Great Britain in 2013
by Dorling Kindersley Limited,
80 Strand, London WC2R 0RL

Penguin Group (UK)
2 4 6 8 10 9 7 5 3
002 – 187176 – March/2013
Copyright © 2013 Dorling Kindersley Limited
All rights reserved.

A CIP catalogue record for this book
is available from the British Library.
ISBN 978-1-4093-6675-1

Printed and bound in China by South China Printing Co Ltd
Discover more at www.dk.com

Introduction

Baby and Toddler Knits Made Easy shows you how to make gorgeous, custom-made, knitted pieces for a child. It provides you with the technical foundation, beautiful patterns, and all the design inspiration you need to create perfect gifts for newborns and toddlers up to three years old.

This beautiful book is suitable for knitters of all skill levels, whether you have only recently decided to take up the craft, or you have years of experience. With more than 50 patterns, including clothing, toys, bits and pieces for the nursery, and accessories, there is something for everyone no matter what your personal taste or level of proficiency.

Throughout the book you are shown ways to experiment with different yarns, colours, embellishments, and fastenings. Have fun choosing the little details that make a design utterly unique to you. If you choose to substitute a yarn, refer to page 202 for a standard equivalent yarn weight chart. Select a yarn of the same weight and one that can also produce the same tension. Remember to knit a tension swatch before you begin a project and adjust your needle size, if necessary, to achieve the tension you need.

When creating anything for a baby or child, safety is paramount: make sure that small pieces are firmly attached and any ribbons and strings are securely fastened or out of reach. Remember to regularly check for wear and tear and repair anything that comes loose.

With *Baby and Toddler Knits Made Easy* you'll find everything you need to knit with confidence and creativity so that you can make hand-knitted projects that will be cherished for years to come. Now the only difficult part will be choosing which pattern to knit first.

Contents

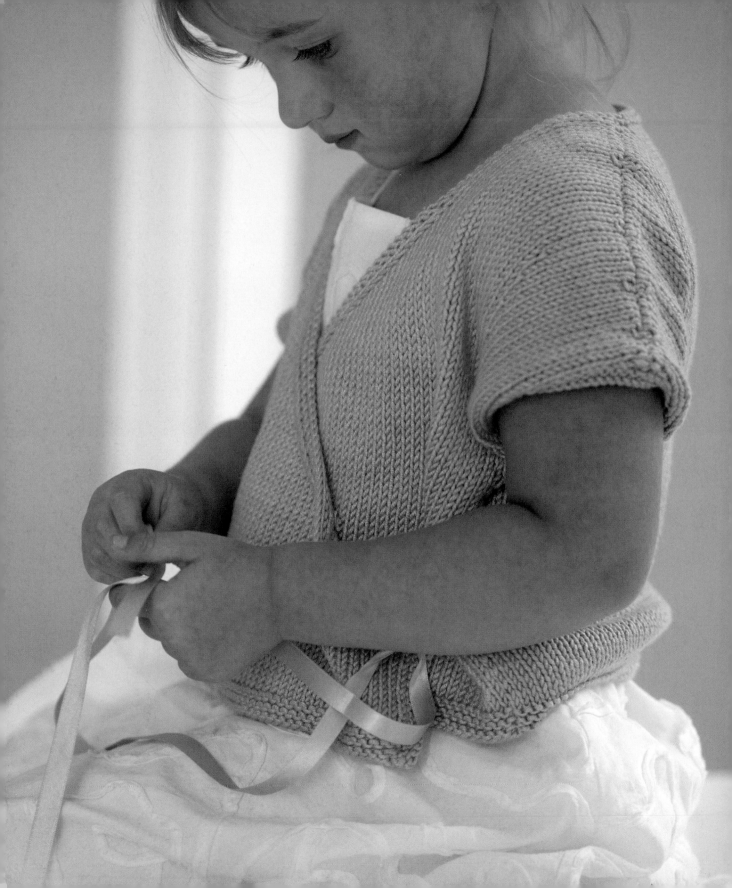

Clothing

🌿 you will need

size

To fit a child, aged 0–3 (3–6:6–12:
12–18:18–24:24–36) months
Actual measurements:
Chest
51 (55:59:63:67:71)cm
(20¼ (22:23:25:26¼:28)in)
Length to shoulder
22 (25:28:32:35:38)cm
(9 (9¾:11:12½:14:15)in)
Sleeve length
15 (17:19:21:23:25)cm
(6 (6¾:7½:8¼:9¼:9¾)in)

materials

Debbie Bliss Eco Baby 50g in
A: White (001) × 2 (2:2:3:3:3)
B: Denim (029) × 2
C: Coral (013) × 1
1 pair of 3mm (UK11/USn/a)
needles
1 pair of 3.25mm (UK10/US3)
needles
2 buttons

tension

25sts and 34 rows to 10cm (4in)
over st st on 3.25mm (UK10/US3)
needles

special abbreviation

wyif (with yarn in front): Leave the
yarn at the front of your work to
make the next stitch rather than
taking it to the back

Striped jumper

THIS CLASSIC, UNISEX JUMPER, striped in white and blue with coral tipping, has a button-neck closure making it easy to pull over baby's head. Knitted in 100 per cent organic cotton yarns that are coloured with non-toxic dyes, this soft jumper is ideal for even the most sensitive skin. Why not try knitting it using different colours or adding novelty buttons?

how to make

Back

With 3mm (UK11/USn/a) needles and yarn C, cast on 66 (70:74:78: 82:86) sts.
1st rib row: K2, [p2, k2] to end.
Cut off yarn C, join on yarn A.
2nd rib row: P2, [k2, p2] to end.
These 2 rows form the rib.
Work a further 8 (8:10:10:12:12) rows.
Change to 3.25mm (UK10/US3) needles.
Beg with a k row, cont in st st and stripes of 6 rows in yarn A and 2 rows in yarn B until back measures 12 (14:16:18:20:22)cm (5 (5½:6¼: 7:8:9)in) from cast on edge, ending with a p row.

Shape armholes

Cont the stripe patt.
Cast off 4sts at beg of next 2 rows.
(58 (62:66:70:74:78) sts)
Next row: K4, skpo, k to last 6sts, k2tog, k4.
Next row: P to end.
Rep the last 2 rows x 9 (10:11:12: 13:14) and the first row again.
(36 (38:40:42:44:46) sts)
Next row: Cast on 2sts, p to end.
Next row: K4, skpo, k to last 8sts, k2tog, k6.

Next row: P to end.
Rep the last 2 rows x 4.
(28 (30:32:34:36:38) sts)
Leave these sts on a spare needle.

Front

With 3mm (UK11/USn/a) needles and yarn C, cast on 66 (70:74:78:82:86) sts.
1st rib row: K2, [p2, k2] to end.
Cut off yarn C, join on yarn A
2nd rib row: P2, [k2, p2] to end.
These 2 rows form the rib.
Work a further 8 (8:10:10:12:12) rows.
Change to 3.25mm (UK10/US3) needles.
Beg with a k row, cont in st st and stripes of 6 rows in yarn A and 2 rows in yarn B until back measures 12 (14:16:18:20:22)cm (5 (5½:6¼: 7:8:9)in) from cast on edge, ending with a p row **.

Shape armholes

Cast off 4sts at beg of next 2 rows.
(58 (62:66:70:74:78) sts)
Next row: K4, skpo, k to last 6sts, k2tog, k4.
Next row: P to end.
Rep the last 2 rows x 9 (10:11:12: 13:14). (38 (40:42:44:46:48) sts)

Shape front neck

Row 1: K4, skpo, k5, k2tog, k1, turn and work on these sts for first side of neck.
Row 2: P to end.
Row 3: K4, skpo, k3, k2tog, k1.
Row 4: P to end.
Row 5: K4, skpo, k1, k2tog, k1.
Row 6: P to end.
Row 7: K4, skpo, k2.
Row 8: P to end.
Row 9: K4, skpo, k1.
Row 10: P to end.
Row 11: K4, skpo. (5sts)
Row 12: P to end.
Leave these sts on a holder.
With RS facing, place centre 10 (12:14:16:18:20) sts on a holder, rejoin yarn to rem sts.
Row 1: K1, skpo, k5, k2tog, k4.

Row 2: P to end.
Row 3: K1, skpo, k3, k2tog, k4.
Row 4: P to end.
Row 5: K1, skpo, k1, k2tog, k4.
Row 6: P to end.
Row 7: K2, k2tog, k4.
Row 8: P to end.
Row 9: K1, k2tog, k4.
Row 10: P to end.
Row 11: K2tog, k4.
Row 12: P to end.
Leave these sts on a holder.

Right sleeve
With 3mm (UK11/USn/a) needles
and yarn C, cast on 30 (30:34:34:
38:38) sts.
1st rib row: K2, [p2, k2] to end.
Cut off yarn C, join on yarn A.
2nd rib row: P2, [k2, p2] to end.
These 2 rows form the rib.
Work a further 10 (10:12:12:14:14)
rows.
Change to 3.25mm (UK10/US3)
needles.
Beg with a k row, cont in st st and

stripes of 6 rows in yarn A and 2
rows in yarn B.
Work 2 rows.
Inc row: K3, M1, k to last 3sts,
M1, k3.
Work 5 rows.
Rep the last 6 rows x 4 (6:7:8:9:11)
and the inc row again.
(42 (46:52:54:60:64) sts)
Cont straight until sleeve measures
15 (17:19:21:23:25)cm (6 (6¾:7½:
8¼:9:9¾)in) from cast on edge,
ending with the same stripe row
as on Back.

Shape sleeve top
Cast off 4sts at beg of next 2 rows.
(34 (38:44:46:52:56) sts)
1st, 2nd, 3rd, and 4th sizes only:
Next row: K4, skpo, k to last 6sts,
k2tog, k4.
Next row: P to end.
Next row: K to end.
Next row: P to end.
Rep the last 4 rows x 2 (1:0:0).
(28 (34:42:44:52:56) sts)***

All sizes:
Next row: K4, skpo, k to last 6sts,
k2tog, k4.
Next row: P to end.
Rep the last 2 rows x 9 (12:15:16:
19:20). (8 (8:10:10:12:14) sts)
Leave these sts on a spare needle.

Left sleeve
Work as given for Right sleeve to
***.
All sizes:
Next row: K4, skpo, k to last 6sts,
k2tog, k4.
Next row: P to end.
Rep the last 2 rows x 3 (6:9:10:
13:14). (20 (20:22:22:24:26) sts)
All sizes:
Mark end of last row with a coloured
thread.
Rep the last 2 rows x 2.
Buttonhole row: K1, k2tog, wyif, k1,
skpo, k to last 6sts, k2tog, k4.
Next row: P to end.
Next row: K4, skpo, k to last 6sts,
k2tog, k4.

Raglan shoulder seams are easy to stitch up, just be sure to match both sides
of your knitting, as in the photo. Use mattress stitch (see p.240) to join your seams,
gently pulling them together.

Ribbed edges in a k2, p2 knit with
contrast-colour edging stretch for a
comfortable fit.

Buttons at the neck make this jumper easy to pull on and off, ideal for babies and children who don't like getting changed. Try some shiny brass buttons for a nautical look.

Next row: P to end.
Rep the last 2 rows × 2. (8 (8:10:10: 12:14) sts)
Leave these sts on a spare needle.

Neckband
Join both right back and right front raglan seams.
With RS facing, using 3mm (UK11/ USn/a) needles and yarn A, k7 (7:9:9:11:13) sts from Left sleeve, k last st tog with first st of Front, k4, pick up and k 8sts down left side of Front neck, k 10 (12:14:16:18:20) sts from front neck holder, pick up and k 8sts up right side of Front neck, k4, k last st tog with first st of Right sleeve, k6 (6:8:8:10:12), k last st tog with first st of Back, k12 (13:14:15:

16:17), k2tog, k13 (14:15:16:17:18). (76 (80:88:92:100:104) sts)
Row 1: P3, [k2, p2] to last 5sts, k2, p3.
Row 2: K3, [p2, k2] to last 5sts, p2, k3.
Row 3: As row 1.
Buttonhole row: K1, k2tog, wyif, rib to end.
Work 3 more rows.
Cut off yarn A.

Edging
With RS facing, starting at coloured thread using yarn C pick up and k 13sts along sleeve edge, k2tog, rib to last 2sts, skpo, pick up and k 13sts down left side of Back to beg of cast on sts.
Cast off in rib.

Making up
Join raglan seams using mattress stitch (see p.240). Join side and sleeve seams. Join under arm seam. (See pp.240–242 for more information on joining seams.) Lap button band under buttonhole band and sew in place. Securely sew on buttons.

Ballet
wrap cardigan

MAKE A LITTLE GIRL FEEL LIKE A BALLERINA in this pink, short-sleeved wrap cardigan with a ribbon tie. Knitted with soft bamboo-blend yarn that's machine-washable, it's the perfect summer cardigan to go over dresses. Make sure you securely attach the ribbon and tie a double bow so that the ribbon does not come undone and become tangled.

how to make

Back

With 3.25mm (UK10/US3) needles, cast on 58 (64:68:74:80) sts.
K 5 rows.
Change to 4mm (UK8/US6) needles. Beg with a k row, work in st st for 26 (32:36:42:46) rows.

Shape sleeves

Cast on 4 (5:6:7:8) sts at beg of next 2 rows. (66 (74:80:88:96) sts)
Work 4 rows.
Next row: K6 (7:8:9:10), M1, k to last 6 (7:8:9:10) sts, M1, k6 (7:8:9:10).

Work 3 rows.
Next row: K7 (8:9:10:11), M1, k to last 7 (8:9:10:11) sts, M1, k7 (8:9:10:11).
Work 3 rows.
Next row: K8 (9:10:11:12), M1, k to last 8 (9:10:11:12) sts, M1, k8 (9:10:11:12).
Work 3 rows.
Next row: K9 (10:11:12:13), M1, k to last 9 (10:11:12:13) sts, M1, k9 (10:11:12:13).
Work 3 rows.
Next row: K10 (11:12:13:14), M1, k to last 10 (11:12:13:14) sts, M1, k10

(11:12:13:14).
Work 3 rows.
Next row: K11 (12:13:14:15), M1, k to last 11 (12:13:14:15) sts, M1, k11 (12:13:14:15).
3rd, 4th, and 5th sizes only:
Work 3 rows.
Next row: K (14:15:16), M1, k to last (14:15:16) sts, M1, k (14:15:16).
5th size only:
Work 3 rows.
Next row: K (17), M1, k to last (17) sts, M1, k (17).
All sizes:

you will need

size

To fit a girl, aged 3–6 (6–12:12–18: 18–24:24–36) months.
Actual measurements:
Chest
51(56:60:65:70)cm
(20¼ (22¼:23½:26:27½)in)
Length to shoulder
21 (24:27:30:33)cm
(8¼ (9½:10½:12:13)in)
Sleeve length
3 (3:4:4:5)cm
(1¼ (1¼:1½:1½:2¼)in)

materials

Sirdar Snuggy Baby Bamboo DK 50g in
Babe (134) x 3 (3:3:4:4)
1 pair of 3.25mm (UK10/US3) needles
1 pair of 4mm (UK8/US6) needles
1m (40in) of ribbon
1 button
Spare knitting needles
Stitch holder

tension

22sts and 28 rows to 10cm (4in) over st st on 4mm (UK8/US6) needles

special abbreviations

wyif: With yarn in front
wyib: With yarn in back
wrap 1 (on a k row): Wyif, s1, wyib, place slipped st back on left hand needle
wrap 1 (on a p row): Wyib, s1, wyif, place slipped st back on left hand needle

Work 3 (5:5:7:7) rows.
(78 (86:94:102:112) sts)

Shape upper arms

Next 2 rows: K to last 4 (5:5:5:6) sts, wrap 1, turn, p to last 4 (5:5:5:6) sts, wrap 1, turn.
Next 2 rows: K to last 9 (10:10: 10:12) sts, wrap 1, turn, p to last 9 (10:10:10:12) sts, wrap 1, turn.
Next 2 rows: K to last 14 (15:16:17:19) sts, wrap 1, turn, p to last 14 (15:16:17:19) sts, wrap 1, turn.

Shape shoulders

Next 2 rows: K to last 20 (22:24:26:29) sts, wrap 1, turn, p to last 20 (22:24:26:29) sts, wrap 1, turn.
Next 2 rows: K to last 26 (29:32:35:39) sts, wrap 1, turn, p to last 26 (29:32:35:39) sts, wrap 1, turn.
Place 26 (29:32:35:39) sts at each end of needle on a spare needle and

centre 26 (28:30:32:34) sts on a 3rd spare needle.

Left front

With 3.25mm (UK10/US3) needles, cast on 58 (64:68:74:80) sts.
K 5 rows.
Change to 4mm (UK8/US6) needles. Beg with a k row, work in st st for 10 (14:16:20:22) rows.

Shape front neck

Row 1: K to last 4 (5:6:7:8) sts, place these sts on a holder, turn.
Row 2: P to end.
Row 3: K to last 3sts, place these sts on same holder, turn.
Row 4: P to end.
Row 5: K to last 2sts, place these sts on same holder, turn.
Row 6: P to end.
Row 7: K to last 3sts, k2tog, k1.
Row 8: P1, p2tog, p to end.
While working the foll rows, cont to dec on each row in the same way as

on rows 7 and 8 until 33 (36:38:41:44) sts have been dec altogether from the neck edge (do not count sts on holder).
Work a further 8 (10:12:14:16) rows.

Shape sleeve

Next row: Cast on 4 (5:6:7:8) sts, work to end.
Work 5 rows.
Next row: K6 (7:8:9:10), M1, work to end.
Work 3 rows.
Next row: K7 (8:9:10:11), M1, work to end.
Work 3 rows.
Next row: K8 (9:10:11:12), M1, work to end.
Work 3 rows.
Next row: K9 (10:11:12:13), M1, work to end.
Work 3 rows.
Next row: K10 (11:12:13:14), M1, work to end.
Work 3 rows.

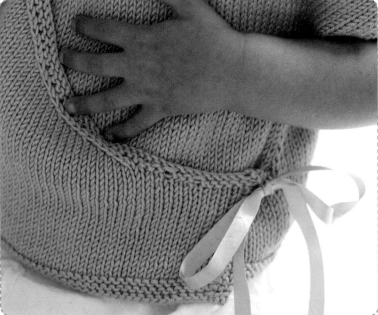

Little, shaped cap sleeves that are smoothly added as you work the body give a soft, pretty feel.

Thread the ribbon through the front and securely tie a double bow. Keep the ribbon short if you're worried about it becoming tangled.

Next row: K11 (12:13:14:15), M1, work to end.
3rd, 4th, and 5th sizes only:
Work 3 rows.
Next row: K (14:15:16), M1, k to end.
5th size only:
Work 3 rows.
Next row: K (17), M1, k to end.
All sizes:
Work 4 (6:6:8:8) rows.
(26 (29:32:35:39) sts)

Shape upper arms
Next row: P to last 4 (5:5:5:6) sts, wrap 1, turn.
K 1 row.
Next row: P to last 9 (10:10:10:12) sts, wrap 1, turn.
K 1 row.
Next row: P to last 14 (15:16:17:19) sts, wrap 1, turn.
K 1 row.

Shape shoulder
Next row: P to last 20 (22:24:26:29) sts, wrap 1, turn.
K 1 row.
Join left upper sleeve and shoulders by knitting one st together from front and back and casting them off (see p.211, Three-needle cast off).

Right front
With 3.25mm (UK10/US3) needles, cast on 58 (64:68:74:80) sts.
K 5 rows.
Change to 4mm (UK8/US6) needles. Beg with a k row, work in st st for 10 (14:16:20:22) rows.

Shape front neck
Row 1: K4 (5:6:7:8), place these sts on a holder, k to end.
Row 2: P to end.
Row 3: K3, place these sts on same holder, k to end.
Row 4: P to end.
Row 5: K2, place these sts on same

holder, k to end.
Row 6: P to end.
Row 7: K1, skpo, k to end.
Row 8: P to last 3sts, p2tog tbl, p1.
While working the foll rows cont to dec on each row in the same way as on rows 7 and 8 until 33 (36:38: 41:44) sts have been decreased altogether (do not count sts on holder).
Work a further 9 (11:13:15:17) rows.

Shape sleeve
Next row: Cast on 4 (5:6:7:8) sts, work to end.
Work 4 rows.
Next row: K to last 6 (7:8:9:10) sts, M1, k6 (7:8:9:10).
Work 3 rows.
Next row: K to last 7 (8:9:10:11) sts, M1, k7 (8:9:10:11).
Work 3 rows.
Next row: K to last 8 (9:10:11:12) sts, M1, k8 (9:10:11:12).
Work 3 rows.
Next row: K to last 9 (10:11:12:13) sts, M1, k9 (10:11:12:13).
Work 3 rows.
Next row: K to last 10 (11:12:13:14) sts, M1, k10 (11:12:13:14).
Work 3 rows.
Next row: K to last 11 (12:13:14:15) sts, M1, k11 (12:13:14:15).
3rd, 4th, and 5th sizes only:
Work 3 rows.
Next row: K to last (14:15:16) sts, M1, k (14:15:16).
5th size only:
Work 3 rows.
Next row: K to last (17) sts, M1, k (17).
All sizes:
Work 5 (7:7:9:9) rows.
(26 (29:32:35:39) sts)

Shape upper arms
Next row: K to last 4 (5:5:5:6) sts, wrap 1, turn.
P 1 row.

Next row: K to last 9 (10:10:10:12) sts, wrap 1, turn.
P 1 row.
Next row: K to last 14 (15:16:17:19) sts, wrap 1, turn.
P 1 row.

Shape shoulder
Next row: K to last 20 (22:24:26:29) sts, wrap 1, turn.
P 1 row.
Join right upper sleeve and shoulders using a three-needle cast off.

Neck edging
With RS facing and 3.25mm (UK10/US3) needles, s9 (10:11:12:13) sts from right front holder onto a needle, pick up and k44 (47:50:53:56) sts up right front, k26 (28:30:32:34) sts from back neck holder, pick up and k44 (47:50:53:56) sts down left front neck, k5 (6:7:8:9), k2tog, yrn, k2 from left front holder.
(132 (142:152:162:172) sts)
K 2 rows.
Cast off.

Sleeve edging
With RS facing and 3.25mm (UK10/US3) needles, pick up and k44 (50:56:62:68) sts from row ends.
K 2 rows.
Cast off.

Front edgings
With RS facing and 3.25mm (UK10/US3) needles, pick up and k10 (13:16:19:21) sts along front edge.
K 2 rows.
Cast off.

Making up
Join sleeve and side seams. Sew ribbon to left seam level with front neck shaping, thread one end through right front to tie. Sew button to right inside seam level with buttonhole.

For *Long, striped hat* see pages 146–149

Dino jumper

A PANEL OF INTARSIA BRONTOSAURUSES make this raglan sleeve jumper a treat for dinosaur-lovers. Knitted in brightly coloured 100 per cent cotton yarn this jumper is soft and easy to wash. You can give your dinosaurs eyes by making a French knot in the centre of each head, use the photograph as your guide.

🌿 you will need

size
To fit a child, aged 2–3 years

materials
Rowan Handknit Cotton
50g in
A: Yacht (357) × 4
B: Gooseberry (219) × 1
C: Rosso (215) × 1
Scrap of black DK weight yarn
1 pair of 4mm (UK8/US6) needles
60cm (24in) long 4mm (UK8/US6) circular needle
Blunt-ended needle

tension
20sts and 28 rows to 10cm (4in) over st st on 4mm (UK8/US6) needles

🌿 how to make

Front
Using 4mm (UK8/US6) needles, cast on 54sts in yarn A.
Row 1: *K2, p2, rep from * to last 2sts, k2.
Row 2: *P2, k2, rep from * to last 2sts, p2.
Rows 3–9: Rep rows 1 and 2.
Change to yarn C.
Row 10: Beg with a purl row inc 6sts across the row. (60sts)
Start intarsia following the Dino chart (see p.22) from row 1 and using yarn B for the dinosaurs.
Row 11: K.
Row 12: P.
Row 13: K.
Row 14: P.
Row 15: K.
Row 16: P1, M1, p to the last st, M1, p1. (62sts)
[Rep rows 11–16 foll the chart] × 5. (72sts)
Please note: On row 31 change to yarn A and cont as stated above. Work 6 more rows in st st starting with a k row, without inc.

Armhole shaping
Row 53: Cast off 2sts at beg of row, k to end. (70sts)
Row 54: Cast off 2sts at beg of row, p to end. (68sts)
Row 55 (start raglan shaping): K1, skpo, k to last 3sts, k2tog, k1. (66sts)
Row 56: P.
[Rep rows 55–56] × 13, then row 55 once up to row 83 inclusive. (38sts)
Row 84 (divide for neck front): P16, p2tog, cast off 2sts, p2tog, p16. (34sts)
Row 85: K1, skpo, k to last 2sts, k2tog.
Row 86: P2tog, p to end
[Rep rows 85–86] × 4.
You will have 2sts on the needle.
Cast off.
Rejoin yarn to rem 17sts with RS facing. Rep as for left side of neck reversing shaping.

Back
Work in the same manner as Front omitting the neck front shaping, and continuing the raglan armhole shaping until there are 28sts on the needle.
Cast off.

Sleeves (Make 2)
Using 4mm (UK8/US6) needles, cast on 32sts in yarn A.
Rows 1–10: *K2, p2, rep from * to end.

Rows 11–14: St st, starting with a k row.
Row 15: K1, M1, k to last st, M1, k1. (34sts)
Rows 16–19: St st, starting with a p row.
Row 20: P1, M1, p to last st, M1, p1. (36sts)
[Rep rows 11–20] x 4, then [rows 11–15] x 1. (52sts)
Row 61: P.
Row 62: K.
Row 63: P.
Row 64 (armhole shaping): Cast off 2sts at beg of row, k to end. (50sts)
Row 65: Cast off 2sts at beg of row, p to end. (48sts)
Row 66 (start of raglan shaping): K1, skpo, k to last 3sts, k2tog, k1. (46sts)
Row 67: P.
Rep rows 66–67 until you have 4sts left.
Cast off.

Collar
Sew the sleeves to the front and back along the raglan edges using mattress stitch (see p.240).

A high, ribbed collar will help keep the cold out on Autumn days. Knitted in 100 per cent cotton yarn the collar won't itch even sensitive skin. The ribbing on the collar echoes the ribbing on the cuffs and bottom edge, which stretch to fit.

Using the 60cm (24in) long 4mm (UK8/US6) circular needle, pick up 19sts up right side of neck, 2sts across the top of the sleeve, 28sts across the back, 2sts across the top of the sleeve and 19sts down left side of neck. (70sts)
Row 1: *K2, p2 rep from * until end of row.
Rows 2–18: Rep row 1.
Cast off.

Making up
Using mattress stitch sew the side and sleeve seams together. Turn the jumper right side out.

Dino chart

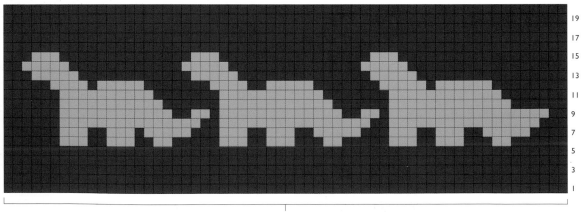

19
17
15
13
11
9
7
5
3
1

60sts

■ Rosso (215)
■ Gooseberry (219)

top tip

See pages 233 –235 for more information about working colourwork.

Flower skirt

MADE IN SIMPLE GARTER STITCH with a stocking stitch waistband and picot edging, this flower motif skirt is easy to put on and comfortable to wear. The 100 per cent cotton yarn will be soft on delicate skin. The flowers are created using bullion stitch (see p.244). You can work a knitted button loop (see p.243) if you would prefer a more robust closure.

you will need

size
To fit a girl, aged 2–3 years

materials
Rowan Handknit Cotton
50g in
A: Raspberry (356) × 4
B: Bleached (263) × 1
C: Celery (309) × 1
1 pair of 4mm (UK8/US6) needles
1 button
Blunt-ended needle

tension
19–20sts and 28 rows to 10cm (4in) over g st on 4mm (UK8/US6) needles

how to make

Skirt (Make 2)
Cast on 50sts in yarn A in st st.

Waistband
Row 1: P.
Row 2: K.
Rows 3–11: Rep rows 1 and 2.
Row 12: *K2tog, M1 (rep from * until end of row).
Rows 13–23: Rep rows 1 and 2.

Main skirt
Cont in yarn A, but change to g st.
Rows 24–26: K.
Row 27: K5, M1, k to last 5sts, M1, k5. (52sts)
Rows 28–93: Rep rows 24–27 until 93 rows knitted in total. (86sts)
Row 94: Picot cast off edge.
*Cast on 3sts, cast off 6sts, rep from * until end of row.

Making up
Fold the waistbands over so that a picot edge is formed by the lace holes and sew in place using backstitch (see p.242), do this reasonably loosely so it still has a bit of give.

Place the two skirt pieces right sides together and sew up each side using mattress stitch (see p.240), on the right hand side leave the waistband side open. Sew the button on the front side of the waistband, on the other side sew a button loop.

Embroidery
Using bullion stitch embroidery technique work 10 daisies with stems along the bottom of the front and back of skirt. Use yarn B for the petals and yarn C for the stems.

Attach the button to the front of the waistband. Create a button loop from the back part of the waistband using a blunt-ended needle and yarn.

Newborn cardigan

THIS SOFT, LUXURIOUS CARDIGAN is perfect for a newborn baby. You only need to know stocking stitch for the body and garter stitch for the yoke, edges, and sleeves. Boys' and girls' buttonholes are worked on different sides, so follow the relevant instructions below. Choose a button to complement your yarn colour choice.

you will need

size
To fit a newborn baby

materials
Rowan Cashsoft DK 50g in Sky pink (540) × 3
1 pair of 3.25mm (UK10/US3) needles
Stitch holder
Large-eyed needle
1 button

tension
27sts and 37 rows to 10cm (4in) over st st on 3.25mm (UK10/US3) needles

how to make

Back
Using cable cast on method, working between stitches, cast on 62sts.
Row 1 (WS): K.
Rows 2 and 3: As row 1.
Row 4 (RS): K.
Row 5: P.
Last 2 rows set st st. Cont working in st st until work measures 17cm (6¾in) from cast on edge, ending with a WS row.

Shape arms
Next 2 rows: Cast on 36sts, k to end. (134sts)
Cont in g st as set for a further 32 rows.

Shape right front
Next row: K57 and turn, leaving rem 77sts on a stitch holder.

Shape neck
Row 1 (WS): K1, skpo, k to end. (56sts)
Row 2 (RS): K to last 3sts, k2tog, k1. (55sts)
Row 3: As row 1. (54sts)

K 11 rows ending with a RS row.
Inc row (WS): K1, M1, k to end. (55sts)
K 3 rows without shaping.
Cont increasing at neck edge as set by inc row on next and foll 3 alt rows, then at neck edge of foll 2 rows. (61sts)
Next row: Cast on and k7, k to end. (68sts)
For a girl only:
Place buttonhole: K to last 5sts, cast off 3sts, k1.
Next row: K2, cast on 3sts, k to end.
For a boy only:
K 2 rows.
For boy and girl:
Shape underarm (RS): Cast off 36sts, k to end.
Row 1 (WS): K5, p to end.
Row 2 (RS): K to end.
Last 2 rows set st st with g st border.
Rep last 2 rows until work measures 16cm (6¼in) from underarm, ending with a RS row.
K 3 rows.
Cast off.

clothing

Shape left front

With RS facing, rejoin yarn to rem sts.
Cast off next 20sts, k to end. (57sts)
Row 1 (WS): K to last 3sts, k2tog, k1. (56sts)
Row 2 (RS): K1, skpo, k to end. (55sts)
Row 3 (WS): As row 1. (54sts)
K 12 rows without shaping, ending with a WS row.
Inc row (RS): K1, M1, k to end. (55sts)
K 2 rows without shaping.

Cont increasing at neck edge as set by inc row on next and foll 3 alt rows, then at neck edge of foll 2 rows. (61sts)
Next row (WS): K.
Next row (RS): Cast on and k7, k to end. (68sts)
For a girl only:
K 2 rows.
For a boy only:
Place buttonhole: K to last 5sts, cast off 3sts, k1.
Next row: K2, cast on 3sts, k to end.
For boy and girl:

Shape underarm (WS): Cast off 36sts, k to end.
Row 1 (RS): K to end.
Row 2 (WS): P to last 5sts, k5.
Rep last 2 rows until work measures 16cm (6¼in) from underarm, ending with a RS row.
K 3 rows.
Cast off.

Making up

Join side and underarm seams using mattress stitch (see p.240). Steam gently and attach the button.

A professional finish can be achieved with the right trimmings and embellishments. The colours in this understated mother of pearl button will blend well with anything.

Garter stitch (see p.215) makes a thick fabric. It is used here on the arms to help keep the baby warm, and also to provide an interesting variation in texture.

Stocking stitch (see p.215) uses only knit and purl stitches and works well in this yarn as it produces a smooth fabric that looks store-bought.

top tip

The garter stitch edging keeps the stocking stitch from curling.

(See p.215)

For *Rattle ball* see pages 100–101

Baby jacket

THIS PRACTICAL, CHUNKY JACKET makes a great cover-up. Knitted in garter stitch, which creates a thick texture, this jacket is warm to wear and quick to knit. The main part of the jacket is knitted in one piece with no side seams. The jacket is a classic style that can also be made for a boy – just choose masculine colours and put the buttons on the opposite side.

🌿 you will need

size

To fit a child, aged 1 (2:3) years
Actual measurements:
Width across back
24 (27:30)cm (9½ (10½:12)in)
Length (shoulder to hem)
29 (32:35)cm
(11½ (12½:13¾)in)
Sleeve (underarm)
18 (20:22)cm (7 (8:9)in)

materials

Debbie Bliss Cashmerino
Aran 50g in
A: Heather (046) × 4 (4:5)
B: Silver (202) × 1 (1:1)
1 pair of 4mm (UK8/US6)
needles
1 pair of 5mm (UK6/US8)
needles
Blunt-ended needle
3 × stitch holders
3 × 22mm (¾in) buttons
Sewing thread to match yarn

tension

17sts and 31 rows to 10cm
(4in) over g st on 5mm
(UK6/US8) needles

🌿 how to make

Back and fronts (In one piece)

With 5mm (UK6/US8) needles and yarn A, cast on 134 (142:149) sts using cable cast on method, working between stitches.
Row 1 (WS): K each st tbl.
Row 2: S1, k to end.
Rep row 2 (knit every row) until work measures 13 (15:17)cm (5¼ (6:6¾)in), ending after a RS row.
Next row: K4 (2:4), [k2tog, k3] × 26 (28:29). (108 (114:120) sts)

Divide for armholes

Next row (RS): K25 (26:28), then transfer these sts, for Right front, to a stitch holder; cast off 7 (8:8), k43 (45:47) and transfer these 44 (46:48) sts, for the Back, to another stitch holder; cast off next 7 (8:8) sts and k to end.

Left front

Cont in g st on these 25 (26:28) sts until work measures 23 (25:28)cm (9 (9¾:11)in) from cast on row, ending at the front edge.

Shape neck

Cast off 6sts at beg of next row, 2sts at beg of next 1 (2:3) alt rows and 1st at beg of next 5 (4:3) alt rows.

(12 (12:13) sts). Cont in g st until work measures 28 (31:34)cm (11 (12¼:13½)in) from cast on row, ending on armhole edge.
Cast off.

Right front

Rejoin yarn to armhole edge of sts on stitch holder and complete, following instructions for Left front but reversing shapings.

Back

Rejoin yarn to sts on stitch holder and cont in g st until work measures 27 (30:33)cm (10½ (12:13)in) from cast on row, ending with RS facing.

Garter stitch creates a thick fabric that is nice and warm, perfect for a little spring or autumn jacket. A decrease row at the waist gives the jacket a slight flare out from underneath where the buttons are placed for a loose, comfortable fit.

Contrast-colour edges frame the jacket, but if you prefer a solid-coloured jacket simply work all in the same colour yarn rather than changing.

Shape neck

Next row (RS): K13 (13:14) and transfer these sts to a stitch holder (or leave them on the needle, if you prefer); cast off 18 (20:20), k to end.
Next row: Working on 13 (13:14) sts for Left back, k11 (11:12), k2tog. (12 (12:13) sts)
Next row: K.
Cast off.

Rejoin yarn to neck edge of sts for Right back; k2tog, k to end. (12 (12:13) sts)
Next row: K.
Cast off.

Sleeves (Make 2)

With 4mm (UK8/US6) needles and yarn B, cast on 39 (41:43) sts using cable cast on method.
Row 1 (WS): K each st tbl.
Row 2: S1, k to end.
Row 3: As row 2.
Change to 5mm (UK6/US8) needles and yarn A, working in g st, inc 1st at each end of every 8th row × 4 (5:5). (47 (51:53) sts)
Cont in g st without further shaping until work measures 19 (21:23) cm (7½ (8¼:9)in) from cast on row.
Cast off.

Button loops (Make 3)

With 4mm (UK8/US6) needles and yarn B, cast on 18sts using cable cast on method. Cast off, knitting each st tbl.

Making up and neckband

Join shoulder seams. With RS facing, and using 4mm (UK8/US6) needles and yarn B, starting at right front neck edge, miss the first 3sts, then pick up and k 4sts on cast off edge, then 15sts up neck edge, 4sts down right back neck edge, 18 (20:20) sts from cast off edge at centre back neck, 4sts up left back edge, 15sts down front neck edge and 4sts on cast off edge at front neck. (64 (66:66) sts)

top tip

Using cable cast on, worked between stitches, gives a firmer edge to your knitting.

Work 10 (12:12) rows in g st, then cast off loosely. Fold neckband to inside and slipstitch edge of neckband to inside edge of neck opening.

Join sleeve seams, starting at cuff and stopping approximately 3.5cm (1⅜in) from top. Join sleeves to armholes (match top edge of sleeve to side edges of armhole and open edge of sleeve seam to base of armhole). Stitch the two short ends of each button loop to one front edge of the jacket and the buttons to the opposite side, about 4–5cm (1½–2in) in from the edge, so that when buttons are fastened, the front edges of the jacket overlap slightly.

Place the button loops on the right front for a girl and the left front for a boy. Stitch the buttons to the opposite side of the jacket. Choose buttons to match your chosen yarn colours: we've used blue shell buttons.

Tiny tank top

THIS PROJECT, KNITTED IN STOCKING STITCH, can be worn on its own in the summer, or as an extra layer when it's chilly outside. Worked in a soft cashmere merino silk 4-ply yarn, it will make a great garment for either a boy or a girl depending on the colours you choose. It has ribbed edges with smart, coloured tipping to match the colour of the stripes.

you will need

size
To fit a child, aged 1 (2:3) years

materials
Sublime Baby Cashmere
Merino Silk 4-ply 50g in
A: Vanilla (003) × 1 (1:2)
B: Sleepy (123) × 1 (1:2)
C: Paddle (100) × 1 (1:1)
1 pair of 3.75mm (UK9/US5)
needles
1 pair of 4mm (UK8/US6)
needles
2 stitch holders and spare
needles
Large-eyed needle

tension
22sts and 28 rows to 10cm
(4in) over st st on 4mm
(UK8/US6) needles

how to make

Back
Using 3.75mm (UK9/US5) needles and yarn B, cast on 62 (66:70) sts.
Rib row 1 (RS): K2, [p2, k2] to end.
Change to yarn A.
Rib row 2: P2, [k2, p2] to end.
These 2 rows form the rib.
Work a further 4 rows, inc 2sts evenly across last row. (64 (68:72) sts)
Change to 4mm (UK8/US6) needles.
Work in stripe patt of [2 rows in yarn B, 4 rows in yarn C, 2 rows in yarn B, 4 rows in yarn A] throughout.
Beg with a k row, cont in st st until back measures 15 (17:19)cm (6 (6¾:7½)in) from cast on edge, ending with a p row.

Shape armholes
Cast off 6sts at beg of next 2 rows.
(52 (56:60) sts)
Next row: K2, skpo, k to last 4sts, k2tog, k2.
Next row: P to end.
Rep the last 2 rows × 3 (4:5).
(44 (46:48) sts)**
Cont in st st until back measures 26 (29:32)cm (10 (11½:12½)in) from cast on edge, ending with a WS row.

Shape back neck
Next row: K12 (12:13), turn and leave rem sts on a spare needle.
Next row: P to end.
Next row: K to last 3sts, k2tog, k1.
Next row: P to end 11 (11:12) sts.
Shape shoulder.
Cast off.
With RS facing, place centre 20 (22:22) sts on a stitch holder, rejoin yarn to rem sts, k to end.
Next row: P to end.
Next row: K1, skpo, k to end.
Next row: P to end 11 (11:12) sts.
Shape shoulder.
Cast off.

Front
Work as given for Back to **.
Cont in st st until front measures 20 (23:26)cm (8 (9¼:10)in) from cast on edge, ending with a WS row.

Shape front neck
Next row: K16 (17:18), turn and leave rem sts on a spare needle.
Next row: P to end.
Next row: K to last 3sts, k2tog, k1.
Next row: P to end.
Rep the last 2 rows × 4 (5:5).
(11 (11:12) sts)

Work straight until front measures same as back to shoulder, ending at armhole edge.
Shape shoulder.
Cast off.
With RS facing, place centre 12sts on a holder, rejoin yarn to rem sts, k to end.
Next row: P to end.
Next row: K1, skpo, k to end.
Rep the last 2 rows × 4 (5:5).
(11 (11:12) sts)
Work straight until front measures same as back to shoulder, ending at armhole edge.
Shape shoulder.
Cast off.

Neckband

Join right shoulder seam.
With 3.75mm (UK9/US5) needles and yarn A, RS facing, pick up and k24 down LS of front neck, k12 from front neck holder, pick up and k24 up RS of front neck, 6sts down RS of back neck, k20 (22:22) sts from back neck holder, inc 2 (4:4) sts evenly across the back neck sts.
Pick up and k6 up RS of back neck.
(94 (98:98) sts)
Next row: P2, [k2, p2] to end.
This row sets the rib.
Work a further 2 rows.
Change to yarn B.
Work 1 row.
Cast off in rib.

Armbands

Join left shoulder and neckband seam.
With 3.75mm (UK9/US5) needles and yarn A, RS facing, pick up and k70 (74:78) sts.
Next row: P2, [k2, p2] to end.
This row sets the rib.
Work a further 2 rows.
Change to yarn B.
Work 1 row.
Cast off in rib.

Making up

Join side and armband seams.
(See pp.240–242 for information on seams.)

top tip

Knit a tension square before you begin to make sure the tank top will fit correctly.

The shoulder seams are joined before the making up process. Join the right shoulder seam before you pick up and knit the neckband and the left shoulder seam before you pick up and knit the armbands.

For an elasticated fit the collar and armholes have a 2 x 2 ribbing (k2, p2 repeat). The stretchy edges make the tank top easy to put on and take off.

Join the seams using a discreet mattress stitch (see p.240). Try to match the stripes as closely as possible for a neat, professional finish.

Tunic dress

WITH ITS SLEEVELESS YOKE AND GATHERED SKIRT, this simple pull-on tunic dress can be worn alone or as a pinafore over a T-shirt or jumper. The skirt section of the tunic is knitted in the round using circular needles. For more information on using circular needles, turn to pages 236–237. Remember to use a stitch marker to keep track of the beginning of your rounds.

you will need

size
To fit a girl, aged 12–18 months (2–3 years)
Actual measurements:
Chest
51 (55)cm (20 (21½)in)
Length (shoulder to hem)
36 (38)cm (14¼ (15)in)
Width across back
27 (29)cm (10½ (11½)in)

materials
Debbie Bliss Cashmerino DK 50g in
Rose pink (042) × 4
60cm (24in) long 4mm (UK8/US6) circular needle
1 pair of 3.25mm (UK10/US3) needles
4 stitch holders (one large, three small)
Blunt-ended needle

tension
20sts and 28 rows to 10cm (4in) over st st on 4mm (UK8/US6) needles

how to make

Please note: When you divide the work for the Front and Back yoke, you can continue to use the circular needle, working back and forth, or change to a pair of straight needles if you prefer.

Skirt
Using a 60cm (24in) long 4mm (UK8/US6) circular needle, cast on 168 (172) sts, join to knit in the round, being careful not to twist sts.
Rounds 1–6: K.
Round 7 (picot hem): [Yo, k2tog] to end of round.
Continue in st st (knit every round) until work measures 24 (26)cm (9½ (10¼)in) (or more, if you wish the dress to be longer).
Next round: [K1, k2tog] to last 0 (1) st, k0 (1). (112 (115) sts)
Work 1 round in st st with no further decreases.

Back yoke
Shape armholes
Row 1: Cast off 3sts, k until there are 53 (54) sts on RH needle and turn, leaving rem sts on a holder for Front yoke.
Row 2: Cast off 3sts, p to end. (50 (51) sts)

Row 3: K1, skpo, k to last 3sts, k2tog, k1. (48 (49) sts)
Row 4: P.
[Rep rows 3 and 4] × 2. (44 (45) sts)
Work 22 (24) rows in st st, ending with RS facing.

Shape shoulders and neck
Next row: Cast off 3sts, k8, k2tog, k1, turn and leave rem sts on a holder.
Next row: P1, p2tog, p to end. (9sts)
Next row: Cast off 3sts, k to last 3sts, k2tog, k1. (5sts)
Next row: P1, p2tog, p to end. Cast off rem 4sts.
Keeping the centre 16 (17) sts on the stitch holder, join yarn to rem 14sts.
Next row: K1, skpo, k to end. (13sts)
Next row: Cast off 3sts, p to last 3sts, p2tog tbl, p1. (9sts)
Next row: K1, skpo, k to end. (8sts)
Next row: Cast off 3sts, p2, p2tog tbl, p1. (4sts)
Cast off rem 4sts.

Front yoke
With RS facing, join yarn to 56 (58) sts on holder.
Row 1: Cast off 3sts, k to end. (53 (55) sts)

Row 2: Cast off 3sts, p to end.
(50 (52) sts)
Row 3: K1, skpo, k to last 3sts, k2tog, k1. (48 (50) sts)
Row 4: P.
[Rep rows 3 and 4] × 2. (44 (46) sts)
Beg with a k row, work 12 (14) more rows in st st.

Shape neck

Row 1: K15 and turn, leaving rem 29 (31) sts on a holder.
Row 2: P1, p2tog, p to end.
Row 3: K to last 3sts, k2tog, k1.
[Rep rows 2 and 3] × 1, then row 2 × 1. (10sts)
Beg with a k row, work 6 rows in st st.

Shape shoulder

Row 1: Cast off 3sts, k to end.
Row 2: P.
[Rep rows 1 and 2] ×1.

Cast off rem 4sts.
Keeping the centre 14 (16) sts on the stitch holder, join yarn to rem 15sts for Right front neck and k to end.
Complete to match Left front neck, reversing shapings.

Armhole bands (Make 2)

With RS facing and using 3.25mm (UK10/US3) needles, pick up and k50 (54) sts around armhole edge, starting and ending at shoulder.
Work 3 rows in k1, p1 rib.
Cast off in rib.

Neckband

Stitch right shoulder seam, including edge of armhole band.
With RS facing and using 3.25mm (UK10/US3) needles, starting at Left shoulder, pick up and k 13sts down left side of neck, k 14 (16) sts from

holder at centre front neck, pick up and k 13sts up right side of neck and k 16 (17) sts from holder at right back neck. (56 (59) sts)
Work 3 rows in k1, p1 rib.
Cast off in rib.

Making up

Fold picot hem to inside on lower edge of skirt and slip stitch in place.

Decreasing when you switch from knitting the skirt section to the yoke section defines these as two different areas, even though they are one piece.

Ribbed armholes and neckline in a k1, p1 pattern stretch to make the garment comfortable around the arms and neck.

A picot hem creates a scalloped design. It is knitted by making a row of yarnover lace holes on stocking stitch and then folding the edge over.

Classic
boy's cardigan

KNITTED IN A SOFT, 4-PLY YARN made from a natural blend of merino wool, silk, and cashmere, this cardigan will feel gentle next to baby's skin while keeping him snug as a bug in a rug. Moss stitch edging adds a more unique feature than ribbing and the prominent v-neck collar gives this cardigan an air of sophistication perfect for the little gentleman.

🍃 you will need

size
To fit a boy, aged 6–12
(12–18:18–24:24–36) months
Actual measurements:
Chest
56 (60:66:72)cm
(22¼ (23½:26:28¼)in)
Length to shoulder
28 (31:34:37)cm
(11 (12¼:13½:14½)in)
Sleeve length
15 (17:19:22)cm
(6 (6¾:7½:9)in)

materials
Sublime Baby Cashmere
Merino Silk 4-ply 50g in
Cuddle (002) x 4 (4:5:5)
1 pair of 3.25mm (UK10/
US3) needles
1 pair of 4mm (UK8/US6)
needles
4 (4:5:5) buttons
Stitch holder

tension
22sts and 28 rows to 10cm
(4in) over st st on 4mm
(UK8/US6) needles

🍃 how to make

Back
With 3.25mm (UK10/US3) needles, cast on 65 (71:77:83) sts.
Row 1: K1, [p1, k1] to end.
This row forms the moss st.
Work a further 7 rows.
Change to 4mm (UK8/US6) needles.
Beg with a k row work in st st until back measures 18 (20:22:23)cm (7 (8:9:9¼)in) from cast on edge, ending with a p row.

Shape raglan armholes
Cast off 5 (6:7:8) sts at beg of next 2 rows. (55 (59:63:67) sts)
Next row: K2, skpo, k to last 4sts, k2tog, k2.
Next row: P to end.
Rep the last 2 rows x 15 (16:17:18).
Cast off rem 23 (25:27:29) sts.

Right front
With 3.25mm (UK10/US3) needles, cast on 35 (38:41:44) sts.
Row 1: [K1, p1] to last 1 (0:1:0) sts, k1 (0:1:0).
Row 2: K1 (0:1:0), [p1, k1] to end.
These 2 rows form the moss st.
Work a further 6 rows.
Change to 4mm (UK8/US6) needles.

Row 1: Moss st 5, k to end.
Row 2: P to last 5sts, moss st 5.
These 2 rows form the st st with moss st edging.
Work straight until front measures 18 (20:22:23)cm (7 (8:9:9¼)in) from cast on edge, ending with a WS row.

Shape raglan armhole
Next row: Moss st 5, place these 5 sts on a holder, k to end.
Next row: Cast off 5 (6:7:8) sts, p to end. (25 (27:29:31) sts)
Next row: K2, skpo, k to last 4sts, k2tog, k2.
Next row: P to end.
Next row: K to last 4sts, k2tog, k2.
Next row: P to end.
Rep the last 4 rows x 5 (6:7:8).
(7 (6:5:4) sts)
Next row: K to last 4sts, k2tog, k2.
Next row: P to end.
Rep the last 2 rows x 3 (2:1:0). (3sts)
Cast off.
Mark position for 4 (4:5:5) buttons, the first on the 5th row of moss st and the 4th (4th:5th:5th) 4 rows below neck shaping, the remaining 2 (2:3:3) spaced evenly between.

Left front

With 3.25mm (UK10/US3) needles, cast on 35 (38:41:44) sts.
Row 1: K1 (0:1:0), [p1, k1] to end.
Row 2: [K1, p1] to last 1 (0:1:0) sts, k1 (0:1:0).
These 2 rows form the moss st.
Work a further 2 rows.
Buttonhole row: Moss st to last 4sts, yrn, work 2 tog, moss st 2.
Work a further 3 rows.
Change to 4mm (UK8/US6) needles.
Row 1: K to last 5sts, moss st 5.
Row 2: Moss st 5, p to end.
These 2 rows form the st st with moss st edging.
Working buttonholes to match markers, work straight until front measures 18 (20:22:23)cm (7 (8:9:9¼)in) from cast on edge, ending with a WS row.

Shape raglan armhole

Next row: Cast off 5 (6:7:8) sts, k to last 5sts, place these 5sts on a holder. (25 (27:29:31) sts)
Next row: P to end.
Next row: K2, skpo, k to last 4sts, k2tog, k2.
Next row: P to end.
Next row: K2, skpo, k to end.
Next row: P to end.
Rep the last 4 rows × 5 (6:7:8).
(7 (6:5:4) sts)
Next row: K2, skpo, k to end.
Next row: P to end.

Rep the last 2 rows × 3 (2:1:0). (3sts)
Cast off.

Sleeves

With 3.25mm (UK10/US3) needles, cast on 37 (39:41:43) sts.
Row 1: K1, [p1, k1] to end.
This row forms the moss st.
Work a further 7 rows.
Change to 4mm (UK8/US6) needles.
Beg with a k row work 2 rows in st st.
Inc row: K3, M1, k to last 3sts, M1, k3.
Work 5 rows.
Rep the last 6 rows × 4 (5:6:7) and the inc row again. (49 (53:57:61) sts)
Cont straight until sleeve measures 15 (17:19:22)cm (6 (6¾:7½:9)in) from cast on edge, ending with a p row.

Shape raglan sleeve top

Cast off 5 (6:7:8) sts at beg of next 2 rows. (39 (41:43:45) sts)
Next row: K2, skpo, k to last 4sts, k2tog, k2.
Next row: P to end.
Rep the last 2 rows × 15 (16:17:18).
Cast off rem 7sts.

Left collar

With 4mm (UK8/US6) needles, cast on 11 (13:17:19) sts. With RS facing, pick up and k31 (33:35:37) sts down left front neck edge, moss st 5 from holder. (47 (51:57:61) sts)
Row 1: Moss st to end.
4th size only:
Next 2 rows: Moss st to last 42sts, turn, sl, moss st to end.
3rd and 4th sizes only:
Next 2 rows: Moss st to last 38sts, turn, sl, moss st to end.
2nd, 3rd, and 4th sizes only:
Next 2 rows: Moss st to last 34sts, turn, sl, moss st to end.
All sizes:
Next 2 rows: Moss st to last 30sts, turn, sl, moss st to end.

Moss stitch edging keeps the stocking stitch body from rolling, while providing a more unusual edge than ribbing.

Next 2 rows: Moss st to last 26sts, turn, sl, moss st to end.
Next 2 rows: Moss st to last 22sts, turn, sl, moss st to end.
Next 2 rows: Moss st to last 18sts, turn, sl, moss st to end.
Next 2 rows: Moss st to last 14sts, turn, sl, moss st to end.
Next 2 rows: Moss st to last 10sts, turn, sl, moss st to end.
Next 2 rows: Moss st to last 6sts, turn, sl, moss st to end.
Next row: Moss st to last 6sts, p3tog, k1, p1, k1.
Next row: Moss st to end.
Next row: Moss st to last 4sts, p3tog, k1.
Cast off in moss st.

Right collar

With 4mm (UK8/US6) needles, s 5sts from holder onto needle, pick

A v-neck and defined raglan sleeve seams, combined with a moss stitch collar, give a masculine feel to this little cardigan.

The button band is knitted in moss stitch. Have fun choosing buttons that go with your yarn colour.

up and k31 (33:35:37) sts up right front neck edge, cast on 11 (13:17:19) sts. (47 (51:57:61) sts)
Next 2 rows: K1, [p1, k1] × 8 (8:9:9), turn, s1, moss st to end.
4th size only:
Next 2 rows: Moss st to last 38sts, turn, s1, moss st to end.
3rd and 4th sizes only:
Next 2 rows: Moss st to last 34sts, turn, s1, moss st to end.
2nd, 3rd, and 4th sizes only:
Next 2 rows: Moss st to last 30sts, turn, s1, moss st to end.
All sizes:
Next 2 rows: Moss st to last 26sts, turn, s1, moss st to end.
Next 2 rows: Moss st to last 22sts, turn, s1, moss st to end.
Next 2 rows: Moss st to last 18sts, turn, s1, moss st to end.
Next 2 rows: Moss st to last 14sts, turn, s1, moss st to end.
Next 2 rows: Moss st to last 10sts, turn, s1, moss st to end.
Next 2 rows: Moss st to last 6sts, turn, s1, moss st to end.
Next row: Moss st to last 6sts, p3tog, k1, p1, k1.
Next row: Moss st to end.
Next row: Moss st to last 4sts, p3tog, k1.
Cast off in moss st.

Making up
Join raglan seams. Join row ends of collar, sew cast on edge to neck edge, easing in fullness. Join side and sleeve seams. Sew on buttons.

top tip
Space the buttons evenly by counting the rows between them.

For *Shoe booties* see pages 156–157

Button-neck jumper

THIS SWEATER IS WORKED WITH SLIPPED STITCHES that create long floats. It is knitted in a lightweight aran, natural-blend yarn. A button-neck opening along the shoulder seams makes it easy to put on and take off. Remember to always knit a tension square to check that your finished garment will fit correctly. Adjust your needle size if necessary (see p.207).

🌱 you will need

size
To fit a child, aged 0–6 months (1–1½:2–3 years)

materials
The Fibre Company Canopy Worsted 50g in
Blue crown x 3 (5:6)
1 pair of 4mm (UK8/US6) needles
1 pair of 4.5mm (UK7/US7) needles
Large-eyed needle
4 x 12mm (½in) buttons

tension
18sts and 28 rows to 10cm (4in) over st st on 4.5mm (UK7/US7) needles

special abbreviations
SM: Stitch marker
wyif: With yarn in front

🌱 how to make

Front
Using 4mm (UK8/US6) needles, cast on 35 (49:57) sts. Work in k1, p1 rib for 2.5cm (1in). Change to 4.5mm (UK7/US7) needles and set patt as follows:
Row 1: K11 (18:22), place SM, [k1, p1] x 2, s5 wyif, [k1, p1] x 2, place SM, k to end.
Row 2: P11 (18:22), slip SM, [p1, k1] x 2, p5, [p1, k1] x 2, slip SM, p to end.
Row 3: K to marker, [k1, p1] x 2, k2, p1tog with float, k2, [k1, p1] x 2, k to end.
Row 4: As row 2.
Work rows 1–4 x 10 (12:14).

Set up yoke
Row 1: [K1, p1] x 3 (2:4), *s5 wyif, [k1, p1] x 2; rep from * to last 2 (0:2) sts, k1, p1.
Row 2: [P1, k1] x 3 (2:3), *p5, [p1, k1] x 2; rep from * to last 2 (0:4) sts, [p1, k1] to end.

Row 3: [K1, p1] x 3 (2:4), *k2, p1tog with float, k2, [k1, p1] x 2; rep from * to last 2 (0:4) sts, [k1, p1] to end.
Row 4: As row 2.
Work yoke patt rows 1–4 x 2 (3:4), then rows 1–3 one time more. On patt row 4, cast off neck sts as follows:
Work 11 (18:22) sts in patt, cast off centre 13sts, work in patt to end. Work each shoulder separately, beg with LH shoulder.
Dec row: Work in patt as set to last 3sts, k2tog, k1.
Work 1 row in patt.
Rep last 2 rows x 2 (2:3).
Keeping in patt, work 1 more complete patt rep (rows 1–4).
Change to 4mm (UK8/US6) needles and work 5 rows k1, p1 rib. Cast off. Work right shoulder to match left shoulder, reversing shaping.

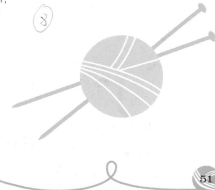

Long floats, made by slipping stitches, create the cable-like pattern on this jumper but without the same level of complication as working cable-knit.

Back

Using 4mm (UK8/US6) needles, cast on 35 (49:57) sts. Work in k1, p1 rib for 2.5cm (1in). Change to 4.5mm (UK7/US7) needles and work in st st to match front length to yoke. Begin yoke patt.

Row 1: [K1, p1] × 3 (2:4), *s5 wyif, [k1, p1] × 2; rep from * to last 2 (0:2) sts, k1, p1.

Row 2: [P1, k1] × 3 (2:4), *p5, [p1, k1] × 2; rep from * to last 2 (0:4) sts, [p1, k1] to end.

Row 3: [K1, p1] × 3 (2:4), *k2, p1tog with float, k2, [k1, p1] × 2; rep from * to last 2 (0:4) sts, [k1, p1] to end.

Row 4: As row 2.

Rep rows 1–4 × 7 (8:9).

Change to 4mm (UK8/US6) needles and work in k1, p1 rib for 2 rows.

Buttonhole row: [K1, p1] × 0 (2:2), k1, yon, k2tog, [p1, k1] × 1 (2:2), yon, k2tog, [p1, k1] × 10 (11:15), p1, k2tog, yon, [k1, p1] × 1 (2:2), k2tog,

yon, [k1, p1] × 0 (2:2), end k1. Work 2 more rows in k1, p1 rib. Cast off.

Sleeves (Make 2)

Using 4mm (UK8/US6) needles, cast on 20 (24:26) sts. Work in k1, p1 rib for 2.5cm (1in). Change to 4.5mm (UK7/US7) needles and work 3 rows in st st.

Inc row: Inc 1st, k to end of row, inc 1st. Rep these 4 rows until you have 32 (36:40) sts. Work even until sleeve measures 15.5 (20:25)cm (6 (8:9¾)in). Cast off all sts.

Making up

Using 4mm (UK8/US6) needles, pick up and k28 (32:34) sts evenly along front neck opening. Work in k1, p1 rib for 5 rows and cast off.

Weave in all ends. Lay front and back flat, face upwards. Place back yoke ribbing over top of front shoulders

The neck is knitted as an open slit without any seams to sew up. Instead, two buttons on either side of the neck opening do the job. Align the buttons to the buttonhole on the opposite side and stitch them in place using a large-eyed needle that fits through the holes of the buttons.

Ribbed edges are not only decorative, but also practical, providing extra stretch to areas where it's needed, such as collars and cuffs.

so ribbing is overlapping. Whip stitch through both layers along 2cm (¾in) of armhole edge. To do this, start with RS facing and the edges together. Insert the large-eyed needle from the RS through the first edge stitch on the right piece and through the first stitch on the left piece from the WS. Pull the yarn through, carry it over the top of the knitting and insert the needle into the next stitch on each piece as before. Repeat this process, taking up 1st from each edge with each stitch. Set in sleeves along armhole edge, and sew side and sleeve seams using mattress stitch (see p.240). Weave in ends and block. Sew buttons on front shoulders to match buttonholes.

top tip

Practise a test square if you're unfamiliar with knitting floats.

Try alternative colours from the suggested yarn type. Here we've used the same yarn in Fern with red gingham patterned buttons. Have fun and create items that match your own unique style.

Cosy hoodie

A UNISEX FIT HOODIE made using a machine-washable, merino wool, silk, cashmere blend yarn for extra cosiness. The yarn comes in a variety of colours, so choose the colour you'd like to work with. Or, try a similar, variegated yarn. Just be sure to knit a tension square and alter your needle size if necessary to make sure your finished hoodie will fit correctly.

you will need

size
To fit a child, aged 6–12 (12–18:18–24:24–36) months
Actual measurements:
Chest
56 (60:66:72) cm
(22¼ (23½:26:28¼)in)
Length to shoulder
28 (31:34:37)cm
(11 (12¼:13½:14½)in)
Sleeve length
15 (17:19:22)cm
(6 (6¾:7½:9)in)

materials
Sublime Baby Cashmere Merino Silk DK 50g in Gooseberry (004) x 4 (5:5:6)
1 pair of 3.25mm (UK10/US3) needles
1 pair of 4mm (UK8/US6) needles

tension
22sts and 28 rows to 10cm (4in) over st st on 4mm (UK8/US6) needles

how to make

Back
With 3.25mm (UK10/US3) needles, cast on 64 (70:76:82) sts.
K 7 rows.
Change to 4mm (UK8/US6) needles. Beg with a k row work in st st until back measures 18 (20:22:23)cm (7 (8:9:9¼)in) from cast on edge, ending with a p row.

Shape armholes
Cast off 5 (6:7:8) sts at beg of next 2 rows. (54 (58:62:66) sts)**
Cont in st st until back measures 28 (30:33:36)cm (11 (12:13:14¼)in) from cast on edge, ending with a p row.

Shape shoulders
Cast off 8 (8:9:9) sts at beg of next 2 rows and 8 (9:9:10) sts at beg of foll 2 rows.
Cast off rem 22 (24:26:28) sts.

Front
Work as given for Back until 18 (20:22:24) rows less have been worked to shoulder shaping.

Divide for front opening
Next row: K24 (26:28:30), p6, k24 (26:28:30).

Next row: P to end.
Rep the last 2 rows once more.
Next row: K24 (26:28:30), M1, p3, turn and work on these sts for first side of front.
Next row: P to end.
Next row: K to last 3sts, M1, p3.
Next row P to end.
Rep the last 2 rows x 5 (6:7:8). (34 (37:40:43) sts)

Shape shoulder
Next row: Cast off 8 (8:9:9) sts, k to last 3sts, M1, p3.
Next row: P to end.
Next row: Cast off 8 (9:9:10) sts, k to last 3sts, p3.
Next row: P to end. (19 (21:23:25) sts)
Leave these sts on a spare needle.
With RS facing, rejoin yarn to rem sts, p3, M1, k to end.
Next row: P to end.
Next row: P3, M1, k to end.
Rep the last 2 rows x 6 (7:8:9). (35 (38:41:44) sts)

Shape shoulder
Next row: Cast off 8 (8:9:9) sts, p to end.
Next row: P3, k to end.
Next row: Cast off 8 (9:9:10) sts, p to end. (19 (21:23:25) sts)

🌿 top tip

For more
information on
tension and
changing
needle sizes,
see page 207.

Hood

Row 1: P3, k1 (3:5:7), [M1, k3] × 5 across sts of left front, cast on 33 (36:39:42) sts, [k3, M1] × 5, k1 (3:5:7), p3 across sts of right front. (81 (88:95:102) sts)

Next row: P to end.

Next row: P3, k to last 3sts, p3.

Rep the last 2 rows until hood measures 22 (24:26:28)cm (9 (9½: 10:11)in), ending with a WS row. Cast off.

Sleeves

With 3.25mm (UK10/US3) needles, cast on 34 (36:38:40) sts.

K 7 rows.

Change to 4mm (UK8/US6) needles. Beg with a k row work 4 rows in st st.

Inc row: K3, M1, k to last 3sts, M1, k3.

Work 5 rows.

Rep the last 6 rows × 4 (5:6:7) and the inc row again. (46 (50:54:58) sts) Cont straight until sleeve measures 15 (17:19:22)cm (6 (6¾:7½:9)in) from cast on edge, ending with a p row. Mark each end of last row with a coloured thread.

Work 6 (6:8:8) rows. Cast off.

Making up

Join right shoulder seams. Matching centre of cast off edge of sleeve to shoulder, sew on sleeves, sewing last 6 (6:8:8) rows to sts cast off at under arm. Join side and sleeve seams. Join back to hood easing in the sts evenly.

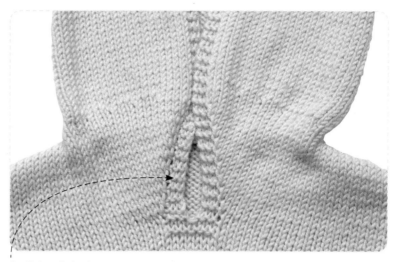

A slight slit in the neckline means the neck will fit loosely and comfortably. The edge is defined by integrally worked garter stitch.

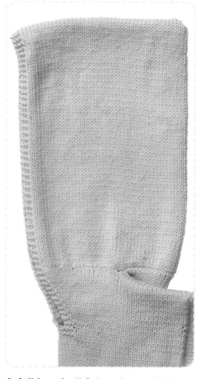

Inset sleeves make this hoddie easy to knit. Sew the underarm to the last few rows of knitting on the body of the jumper.

A full hood will fit loosely over baby's head and even provide enough room for a hat to fit comfortably underneath.

Garter stitch edging keeps the stocking stitch from rolling and provides a nice thick texture on edges.

Robot jumper

A PLAYFUL INTARSIA ROBOT decorates the front of this jumper knitted using a 100 per cent cotton yarn. Colourful moss stitch edging nicely frames the jumper and ties in the colours used for the robot. If you'd like, you can make your robot a small pom-pom hat to stitch on the top of his head. Refer to pages 233–235 for more information on knitting intarsia.

🌿 you will need

size
To fit a child, aged 2–3 years

materials
Rowan Handknit Cotton
50g in
A: Thunder (335) × 4
B: Florence (350) × 1
C: Ochre (349) × 1
D: Atlantic (346) × 1
1 pair of 4mm (UK8/US6)
needles
60cm (24in) long 4mm (UK8/
US6) circular needle
Blunt-ended needle
2 buttons

tension
19–20 sts and 28 rows to
10cm (4in) st st on 4mm
(UK8/US6) needles

🌿 how to make

Jumper front
Using 4mm (UK8/US6) needles cast on 54sts in yarn D.
Row 1: *K1, p1, rep from * to end.
Row 2:*P1, k1, rep from * to end.
Rows 3–9: Rep rows 1 and 2.
Change to yarn A and cont as foll:
Row 10: Beg with a p row inc 6sts (every 9sts) across the row. (60sts)
Start working the robot intarsia in moss st following the Robot chart on p.60, (plain colour borders in st st are worked before the intarsia at the start of each row once the inc starts). At the same time, work the foll:
Rows 11–15: St st, apart from the moss st robot, starting with a k row.
Row 16: P1, M1, p then work moss st robot, p to last st, M1, p1. (62sts)
[Rep rows 11–16] × 5. (72sts)
With yarn A, work 6 more rows of st st border and graph, starting with a k row, without inc.

Armhole shaping
Cont to work intarsia robot in moss st to row 55.
Row 53: Cast off 2sts at beg of row, k to end. (70sts)
Row 54: Cast off 2sts at beg of row, p to end. (68sts)

Row 55 (start raglan shaping): K1, skpo, k to last 3sts, k2tog, k1. (66sts)
Row 56: P.
[Rep rows 55 and 56] × 13 then row 55 once up to row 83 inclusive. (38sts)
Row 84 (divide for neck front): P16, p2tog, cast off 2sts, p2tog, p16. (34sts)
Row 85: K1, skpo, k to last 2sts, k2tog.
Row 86: P2tog, p to end.
[Rep rows 85 and 86] × 4. (2sts)
Cast off.
Rejoin yarn to rem 17sts with RS facing. Rep as for left side of neck reversing shaping.

Back
Work in the same manner as Front omitting the neck front shaping and the intarsia Robot chart, ending after row 83.
Row 84: P18, cast off 2sts, p to end.
Work each side of the back seam separately.
Row 85: K1, skpo, k to end. (17sts)
Row 86: P.
[Rep rows 85 and 86] x 4. (13sts)
Cast off.
Join yarn A to the rem sts with RS facing.
Row 85: K to last 3sts, k2tog, k1. (17sts)
Row 86: P to end.
[Rep rows 85 and 86] x 4. (13sts)
Cast off.

Sleeves (Make 2)
Using 4mm (UK8/US6) needles cast on 32sts in yarn C.
Row 1: *K1, p1, rep from * until end.
Row 2: *P1, k1, rep from * until end.
Rows 3–10: Rep rows 1 and 2.
Change to yarn A and cont as foll:
Rows 11–14: St st, starting with a k row.
Row 15: K1, M1, k to last st, M1, inc 1st, k1. (34sts)
Rows 16–19: St st, starting with a p row.
Row 20: P1, M1, p to last st, M1, p1. (36sts)
[Rep rows 11–20] x 4, then [rows

Robot chart

Background stitches are worked in stocking stitch, robot motif is worked in stitches and colours as key shown below.

- M1
- K2tog on k rows, p2tog on p rows
- Skpo on k rows, ssp on p rows
- K a on RS row, p on a WS row
- P on a RS row, k on a WS row
- Florence (350)
- Atlantic (346)
- Ochre (349)

11–15] × 1. (52sts)

Row 61: P.

Row 62: K.

Row 63: P.

Row 64 (armhole shaping): Cast off 2sts at beg of row, k to end. (50sts)

Row 65: Cast off 2sts at beg of row, p to end. (48sts)

Row 66 (start of raglan shaping): K1, skpo, k to last 3sts, k2tog, k1. (46sts)

Row 67: P.

Rep rows 66 and 67 until 4sts rem. Cast off.

Collar

Join shoulder seams and sleeves together by placing front and back of jumper RS together and sewing together using mattress stitch (see p.240).

Using the 60cm (24in) long 4mm (UK8/US6) circular needle, with the RS facing pick up 68sts evenly around the neck, starting at the left hand centre back, and ending at the right hand centre back.

Row 1: *K1, p1 rep from *until end.

Row 2: *P1, k1 rep from * until end.

Row 3–6: Rep row 1 and 2.

Cast off in moss st.

Buttonhole band

With yarn D, pick up 14sts along the left back centre spilt.

Row 1: *K1, p1, rep from * to end.

Row 2: *P1, k1, p2tog, yrn*, rep from * to *, [p1, k1] to end.

Row 3: *K1, p1, rep from * to end.

Row 4: *P1, k1, rep from * to end.

Cast off in moss st.

Button band

With yarn D, pick up 14sts along the right back centre spilt.

Row 1: *K1, p1, rep from * to end.

Row 2: *P1, k1, rep from * to end.

Rep rows 1 and 2.

Cast off in moss st.

Making up

Sew the side and sleeve seams together. Turn the jumper inside out. Sew end of button and buttonhole bands down. Sew two buttons on button band to match buttonholes. Embroider a face on the robot using the embroidery stitches on pp.244–245.

A two button opening at the back makes it easy to get the jumper over your toddler's head. Choose buttons you feel will complement your jumper. Bright orange or yellow, to match the robot, would be a fun combination.

Contrast-colour moss stitch edges frame the jumper and add a playful feel. You can knit all the edges in different colours from what we've chosen, just substitute the yarn you'd like to use in the correct part of the pattern.

Daisy dress

THIS SQUARE-NECK DRESS is decorated with openwork cluster stitch and embroidered daisies. Knitted in a soft, summer-weight, cotton-blend yarn, it's a great dress for a summer party. For a more colourful approach, work the daisies in multiple colours using scraps of DK-weight yarn. French knots at the centre of each daisy would make a nice touch.

how to make

Back
Using 4mm (UK8/US6) needles and yarn A, cast on 86 (91:103:109) sts.
K I row.
Work openwork patt as follows:
Row I (WS): K.
Row 2: KI, *[kI wy3] × 4 (4:5:5), kI; rep from * to end.
Row 3: KI, *work cluster st over 4 (4:5:5) sts, kI; rep from * to end.
Rows 4 and 5: K.
Beg with a k row, work 3 rows of st st then rep rows I–5 of openwork patt.
Cont to work in st st until the work measures 20 (22:25:27)cm (8 (9:

9¾:10½)in) from cast on edge, ending on a WS row.
Dec row (RS): [K2tog, kI] × 3 (6:6:6), k2tog to last 9 (15:15:19) sts, [kI, k2tog] to last 0 (0:0:1) sts, k0 (0:0:1).
(46 (51:57:61) sts)
3rd size only:
Next row (WS): K2tog, k to last 2sts, k2tog. (55sts)
1st, 2nd, and 4th sizes only:
Next row (WS): K.
All sizes: Work daisy st from rows 2–5. Cont working in st st for 6 (6:8:10) rows, ending on a WS row.
Shape armhole and back opening.

Right back
Row I (RS): Cast off 2 (2:3:3) sts then k until you have 23 (26:27:30) sts on RH needle, turn, leave rem sts on spare needle and work each side separately.
Next row (WS): K4, p to end; this sets up 4st buttonband at centre back worked in g st.
Dec 1st at armhole edge on the next 3 rows. (20 (23:24:27) sts)
Cont working without shaping until armhole measures 8 (9:10:11)cm (3 (3½:4:4¼)in) from beg of shaping, ending on RS row.

you will need

size
To fit a baby, aged 3 (6:12:18) months

materials
Sirdar Calico DK 50g in
A: Muslin (724) × 3
B: Parasol (734) × 1
I pair of 4mm (UK8/US6) needles
I pair of 3.5mm (UKn/a/US4) needles

80cm (32in) long 3.5mm (UKn/a/US4) circular needle
4 × 1cm (½in) buttons
Stitch holder and spare needle
Large-eyed needle

tension
22sts and 31 rows to 10cm (4in) over st st on 4mm (UK8/US6) needles

special abbreviations
wyif: With yarn in front
wy3: Wrap yarn 3 times around the needle, instead of just once, for each stitch
cluster st: Wyif, [slip next st, dropping extra wraps] × 4 (4:5:5), [bring yarn to back between needles, slip 5sts back to LH needle, bring yarn to front between needles, slip 5sts to RH needle] × 2

Choose buttons that blend in, or stand out. We've used shell buttons in purple to match our daisies.

The openwork cluster stitches make a pretty scalloped hem. Try to keep the tension the same for each wrap. Be careful not to pull the yarn too tightly when wrapping.

Lazy daisies (see p.244) decorate the stocking stitch background. Try working daisies in multiple colours, even add beads in the centre if you wish.

Shape back neck
Next row (WS): Cast off 12 (13:13:14) sts.
Cont without shaping on rem 8 (10:11:13) sts for a further 6 rows, ending on a WS row.
Cast off.

Left back
With RS facing, rejoin yarn and cast on 4sts (buttonhole band), k to end of row. (25 (27:29:32) sts)
Cast off 2 (2:3:3) sts at beg of WS row, p to last 4sts, k4; this sets up buttonhole band worked in g st as for Right back.
Dec 1st at armhole edge on next 3 rows. (20 (22:23:26) sts)
At beg of next RS row work buttonhole as follows: K1, k2tog, yon. Work buttonhole in this way on next 2 foll 8th (8th:10th:12th) rows.
Complete to match first side casting off for back neck on RS row.

Front
Work as for the Back until the start of the armhole shaping.
Row 1 (RS): Cast off 2 (2:3:3) sts at the start of the next 2 rows.
Dec 1st at each edge on next 3 rows. (36 (41:43:49) sts)
Work 13 (13:19:19) rows straight, ending on a WS row.

Shape front neck
Next row (RS): K across 8 (10:11:13) sts, turn, leave rem sts on a holder and complete each side separately. Cont without shaping until the front matches the back shoulder ending on a WS row.
Cast off.
With RS facing, rejoin yarn to rem sts and cast off centre 20 (21:21:23) sts, k to end of row. Complete to match first side.

Sleeves (Make 2)
Using 3.5mm (UKn/a/US4) needles and yarn A, cast on 43 (43:47:47) sts.

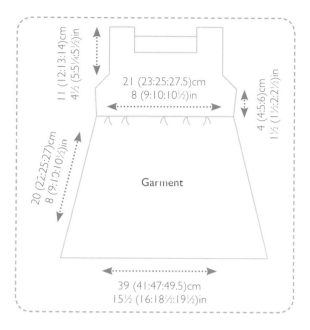

11 (12:13:14)cm
4½ (5:5¼:5½)in

21 (23:25:27.5)cm
8 (9:10:10½)in

4 (4:5:6)cm
1½ (1½:2:2½)in

20 (22:25:27)cm
8 (9:10:10½)in

Garment

39 (41:47:49.5)cm
15½ (16:18½:19½)in

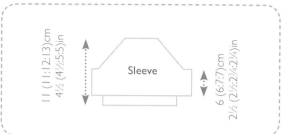

11 (11:12:13)cm
4½ (4½:5:5)in

Sleeve

6 (6:7:7)cm
2½ (2½:2¾:2¾)in

For a perfect fit refer to the garment sizing diagrams. Measure an existing garment that fits your baby well and base your sizing on that. If your baby is between two of the sizes, make the larger size so that the dress will fit for longer and your hard work will not be in vain.

Work 6 rows of k1, p1 rib.
Next row (inc row): Rib 4, M1, *rib 3, M1; rep from *, end rib 3 (3:4:4). (56 (56:61:61) sts)
Change to 4mm (UK8/US6) needles and work rows 1–5 of daisy st.
Cont in st st, work 4 (4:6:6) rows, ending on a WS row.

Shape sleeve head
Cast off 3sts at beg of next 2 rows. (50 (50:55:55) sts)
Dec 1st at each end of next 7 (7:5:5) rows. (36 (36:45:45) sts)
Then dec 1st at each end on every foll alt row until 28 (30:29:27) sts remain. Cast off.

Complete dress
Sew up shoulder seams. Join side seams, being careful to match patt bands. Using the photograph as a guide, embroider daisies onto the dress and sleeves, adding as many or as few as you like. To create the daisies, use a wide-eyed needle and yarn B. See

p.244, Lazy daisy stitch for information on working the daisies. If you wish, you can work a French knot in a contrasting colour at the centre of each daisy.

Sew up sleeve seam
Set in sleeves, matching the centre of each sleeve to the shoulder seam and the underarm seam to the side seam of dress.

Neckband
Using 80cm (32in) long 3.5mm (UKn/a/US4) circular needle, with RS facing and starting at the top of the buttonhole band, pick up and k10 (12:12:12) sts to corner, pick up and k1 from corner, pick up and k16 (18:18:18) sts to front, pick up and k1 from corner, pick up and k18 (19:19:21) sts across front neck, then pick up and k1 from corner, pick up and k16 (18:18:18) sts to back neck, pick up and k1 from corner and finally pick up and k10 (12:12:12) sts to end. (74 (83:83:85) sts)
Row 1 (WS): K10 (12:12:12), p1, k16

(18:18:18), p1, k18 (19:19:21), p1, k16 (18:18:18), p1, k10 (12:12:12).
Row 2: K8 (10:10:10), skpo, k1, k2tog, k12 (14:14:14), skpo, k1, k2tog, k14 (15:15:17), skpo, k1, k2tog, k12 (14:14:14), skpo, k1, k2tog, k to end.
Row 3: K9 (11:11:11), p1, k14 (16:16:16), p1, k16 (17:17:19), p1, k14 (16:16:16), p1, k9 (11:11:11).
Row 4: K1, yon, k2tog, k4 (6:6:6), skpo, k1, k2tog, k10 (12:12:12), skpo, k1, k2tog, k12 (13:13:15), skpo, k1, k2tog, k10 (12:12:12) skpo, k1, k2tog, k7 (9:9:9).
Row 5: K8 (10:10:10), p1, k12 (14:14:14), p1, k14 (15:15:17), p1, k12 (14:14:14), p1, k8 (10:10:10).
Row 6: Cast off.

Making up
Sew in all loose ends. Attach the four buttons to the neckband and buttonband opposite the buttonholes. Block lightly according to the instructions on the ballband.

Toys

Comforter dog

THIS COMFORTER DOG is created using a simple garter stitch and stocking stitch pattern. Its blanket body and soft floppy ears are sure to become a favourite for your little one to hold on to, just like a muslin. We've used 100 per cent organic cotton yarn, which means it is easy to wash, non-toxic, and soft against baby's skin.

🍃 you will need

size
20cm (8in) tall

materials
Debbie Bliss Eco Aran 50g in
A: Gentle (32) × 1
B: Rice cake (31) × 1
C: Duck egg (26) × 1
D: Wellbeing (30) × 1
1 pair of 4mm (UK8/US6) needles
1 pair of 4.5mm (UK7/US7) needles
Toy filling
Scrap of black yarn for eyes, nose, and mouth

tension
18sts and 24 rows to 10cm (4in) over st st on 4.5mm (UK7/US7) needles

🍃 how to make

Head (Make 2)
With 4mm (UK8/US6) needles and yarn A, cast on 6sts.
Rows 1 and 2: K to end.
Row 3: K1, M1, k to last st, M1, k1.
Row 4: K to end.
Rep rows 3 and 4 × 2. (12sts)
Work 8 rows g st.
Next row: Skpo, k to last 2sts, k2tog.
Next row: K to end.
Rep these 2 rows × 2.
Cast off.

Nose
With 4mm (UK8/US6) needles and yarn B, cast on 6sts
Rows 1 and 2: K to end.
Row 3: K1, M1, k to last st, M1, k1.
Row 4: K to end.
Rep rows 3 and 4 once more.
Work 4 rows g st.
Next row: Skpo, k to last 2sts, k2tog.
Next row: K to end.
Rep these 2 rows once more.
Cast off.

Ears (Make 2)
With 4mm (UK8/US6) needles and yarn A, cast on 6sts.
Next row: K1, M1, k to last st, M1, k1.

Work 15 rows g st.
Next row: Skpo, k to last 2sts, k2tog.
Work 9 rows g st.
Next row: Skpo, k to last 2sts, k2tog.
Work 9 rows g st.
Cast off.

Arms (Make 2)
With 4mm (UK8/US6) needles and yarn A, cast on 12sts.
Work 16 rows g st.
Next row: Skpo, k to last 2sts, k2tog.
Next row: K to end.
Rep these 2 rows × 3. (4sts)
Cast off.

Blanket
With 4.5mm (UK7/US7) needles cast on 22sts in yarn B and 22sts in yarn C.
Working in colour and using the intarsia technique, crossing colours where they meet (see p.235), work 6 rows g st. Then k 26 rows st st, knitting the first and last 6 sts of each row to maintain the g st border. Change to yarn D and yarn A. Work a further 26 rows st st, knitting the first and last 6 sts of each row. K 6 rows g st. Cast off in colour.

Making up

Carefully work in the loose yarn tails (see p.242).

Head

Lay down back of head, RS up. Lay the two ears in position on top with cast off edge outermost, in line with outer edge of back of head. Lay front of head on top, with RS down, sandwiching the ears in between. Pin then backstitch (see p.242) around edge leaving neck open. Turn through and stuff. Sew nose piece to front of head, gathering it a little all around the edge. Stuff nose just before closing completely.

Arms

Fold arm in half lengthways, RS together and sew edges together along length. Gather around straight end and secure. Turn through and stuff. Repeat for second arm piece.

Pin head in centre of blanket with face in line with the corner of the yarn C square and stitch in place from below. Stitch arms in position at centre of squares either side (see photograph, below).

Embroider the eyes, nose, and mouth using the photograph, far right, as a guide.

As with all toys, make sure small pieces are securely attached and will not come off. Regularly check toys for wear and tear and repair them if necessary.

top tip

When working the blanket, cross the yarns to prevent holes.
(See p.235)

The blanket body is knitted in one piece using four different coloured yarns in intarsia technique. The dog's head and arms are then discreetly stitched in place in the centre.

Backstitch the two sides of the dog's head together, sandwiching the ears between the two halves. The nose is knitted as a separate piece, attached to the head, and then stuffed.

The blanket body is created using a simple intarsia technique. Stitch the dog's head and arms in place from below. Make sure that all of the pieces are evenly centred on the blanket.

Embroider the eyes, nose, and mouth using scraps of black yarn and a large-eyed sewing needle. Use the photograph, above, as a guide. See satin stitch on p.244 to create the nose.

Your baby will enjoy using the comforter to sooth herself, as she would a muslin. The yarn we used is dyed using non-toxic dyes so it's safe to go in baby's mouth. Be sure to follow the washing instructions on the label of your yarn to avoid any problems when cleaning the comforter.

Cuddly friends

SUITABLE FOR NEWBORNS AND OLDER BABIES, these stylized tiny cot toys are quick to knit. The toys are worked in stocking stitch and garter stitch with embroidered detailing. When sewing on small pieces to any toy, make sure they are securely attached and cannot be pulled off by a young child. Check toys regularly to make sure nothing has loosened.

Friendly penguin

🍃 you will need

size
Approximately 11 x 6.5cm
(4¼ x 2½in)

materials
Sublime Baby Cashmere
Merino Silk DK 50g in
A: Vanilla (003) x 1
B: Button (051) x 1
C: Giallo medio (303) x 1
1 pair of 3.25mm (UK10/
US3) needles
Large-eyed needle
Water-soluble pen
60cm (23½in) length of black
DK yarn
Toy filling
Spray bottle (optional)

tension
22sts and 28 rows to 10cm
(4in) over st st on 3.25mm
(UK10/US3) needles

🍃 how to make

The body and head are knitted together working from the base to the top of the head.

Front
Cast on 20sts in yarn A.
Work 12 rows in st st beg with a k row.
Next row: K1, k2tog, k to last 3sts, ssk, k1. (18sts)
Work 5 rows in st st beg with a p row.
Next row: K1, k2tog, k to last 3sts, ssk, k1. (16sts)
Next row: P.
Break yarn A and join yarn B.
Work 8 rows in st st beg with a k row.
Next row: K2, k2tog, k to last 4sts, ssk, k2. (14sts)
Next row: P.
Rep last 2 rows once more. (12sts)
Next row: K2, k2tog, k to last 4sts, ssk, k2. (10sts)
Next row: P2tog, p to last 2sts, p2tog. (8sts)
Cast off.

Back
Cast on 16sts in yarn B.
Row 1: Inc 1st, k to last 2sts, inc 1st, k1. (18sts)
Next row: P.
Rep last 2 rows once more. (20sts)
Next row: K1, k2tog, k to last 3sts, ssk, k1. (18sts)
Next row: P.

Centre the wings and attach them evenly on both sides of the body, oversewing them in place.

Oversew around the edges of the feet, turn RS out then oversew in place. Make sure they are securely attached.

Sew the beak in place, making sure that the seam runs along the bottom side of the beak and is not visible.

Rep last 2 rows once more. (16sts)
Next row: Cast on 2sts, k to end. (18sts)
Next row: Cast on 2sts, p to end. (20sts)
Work 10 rows in st st beg with a k row.
Next row: K1, k2tog, k to last 3sts, ssk, k1. (18sts)
Work 5 rows in st st beg with a p row.
Next row: K1, k2tog, k to last 3sts, ssk, k1. (16sts) .
Work 9 rows in st st beg with a p row.
Next row: K2, k2tog, k to last 4sts, ssk, k2. (14sts)
Next row: P.
Rep last 2 rows once more. (12sts)
Next row: K2, k2tog, k to last 4sts, ssk, k2. (10sts)
Next row: P2tog, p to last 2sts, p2tog. (8sts)
Cast off.

Feet (Make 2)
Cast on 6sts in yarn C.
Work 4 rows in st st beg with a k row.

Next row: K2tog, k2, ssk. (4sts)
Next row: P.
Next row: K1, M1, k2, M1, k1. (6sts)
Work 4 rows in st st beg with a p row.
Cast off knitwise (on WS of work).

Wings (Make 2)
Cast on 10sts in yarn B.
Row 1: K.
Next row: K2, p to last 2sts, k2.
Rep last 2 rows once more.
Next row: K2, k2tog, k2, ssk, k2. (8sts)
Next row: K2, p4, k2.
Next row: K2, k2tog, ssk, k2. (6sts)
Next row: K2, p2, k2.
Next row: K1, k2tog, ssk, k1. (4sts)
Next row: K.
Next row: K2tog, ssk. (2sts)
Next row: K2tog.
Break yarn and pull through rem st.

Beak
Cast on 10sts in yarn C.
Work 2 rows in st st beg with a k row.
Next row: K2, k2tog, k2, ssk, k2.

(8sts)
Next row: P.
Next row: K1, k2tog, k2, ssk, k1. (6sts)
Next row: P.
Next row: K1, k2tog, ssk, k1. (4sts)
Next row: [P2tog] × 2. (2sts)
Next row: K2tog.
Break yarn and pull through rem st.

Making up
Join the side seams of the penguin using mattress stitch (see p.240) and yarn B, leaving a gap at the top of the head. Turn the penguin inside out and oversew the base to the lower edge of the front. Turn the penguin RS out again. Make sure all yarn tails are secure and on the inside of your toy. Stuff fairly lightly with toy filling. Sew the top of the head using mattress stitch.

Oversew along the top of each wing, attaching them evenly on both sides of the body.

Fold the feet pieces in half
widthways, with the right side on the
inside, and oversew round the sides.
Turn the feet RS out and oversew in
place, stitching along both the upper
and lower edges.

Fold the beak piece in half
lengthways, with the RS on the
inside, and oversew the seam. Turn
the beak RS out and stuff it lightly.
Oversew in place so that the cast on
edge of the beak forms a circle at the
bottom of the face. The seam of the
beak should be on the underside.

Using the photograph on page 73 as
a guide, draw on the penguin's eyes
using the water-soluble pen. Using a
doubled strand of black yarn, work
two French knots for the eyes,
winding your yarn three times
around the needle to make each
knot. Spray the toy lightly to remove
the pen marks and leave to dry.

Little lamb

🌱 you will need

size
Approximately 14.5 x 6.5cm
(6 x 2½in)

materials
Sublime Baby Cashmere
Merino Silk DK 50g in
A: Muffin (278) x 1
B: Vanilla (003) x 1
1 pair of 3.25mm (UK10/
US3) needles
1 pair of 4mm (UK8/US6)
needles
Large-eyed needle
Water-soluble pen
Short length of dark grey
4-ply yarn or dark grey
embroidery thread
Toy filling
Spray bottle (optional)

tension
22sts and 28 rows to 10cm
(4in) over st st on 3.25mm
(UK10/US3) needles

🌱 how to make

The body and head are knitted
together working from the base
to the top of the head.

Body and head (Make 2)
Using 3.25mm (UK10/US3) needles
and yarn A, cast on 18sts.
K 34 rows.
Break yarn A and join yarn B.
Work 10 rows in st st.
Next row: K2, k2tog, k to last 4sts,
ssk, k2. (16sts)
Next row: P2tog, p to last 2sts,
p2tog. (14sts)
Rep last 2 rows once more. (10sts)
Cast off.

Ears (Make 2)
Using 3.25mm (UK10/US3) needles
and yarn B, cast on 10sts.
Row 1: P.
Row 2: K1, k2tog, k4, ssk, k1. (8sts)

Row 3: P2tog, p4, p2tog. (6sts)
Row 4: K1, k2tog, ssk, k1. (4sts)
Row 5: [P2tog] x 2. (2sts)
Row 6: K2tog. (1st)
Break yarn and pull through rem st.

Forelock
Using 4mm (UK8/US6) needles and
yarn A, cast on 5sts.
Row 1: Inc 1st, k2, inc 1st, k1. (7sts)
K 2 rows.
Next row: K2tog, k3, ssk. (5sts)
Cast off.

Making up
Join the side seams and top seam
of the lamb using mattress stitch
(see p.240) and matching yarns.
Make sure all yarn tails are secure
and on the inside of your toy. Stuff
fairly lightly with toy filling. Sew the
lower edge using mattress stitch.

Oversew the ears to the top of the
head. Make sure both ears are evenly
placed on either side so that the head
does not look crooked. The seams
should be at the front of the ears.

Secure the forelock in place by
working a circle of running stitches
around the edge. Make sure the
forelock is centred on top of the head.
If you have any problems, start again.

Fold the ears in half lengthways with the RS on the outside. Oversew the seam close to the edge and the ears in place so that the seams are at the front of the ears. Secure forelock in place by working a circle of running stitch around the edge.

Using the photograph, right, as a guide, draw on the lamb's features using the water-soluble pen. Using dark grey yarn or embroidery thread, work French knots for the eyes. Use yarn or thread double and wind it twice around the large-eyed needle when making the French knot. Embroider three straight stitches in a ''Y'' shape for the nose and mouth. Spray the toy lightly to remove the pen marks and leave to dry.

top tip

Give the toys different expressions by varying your embroidery.

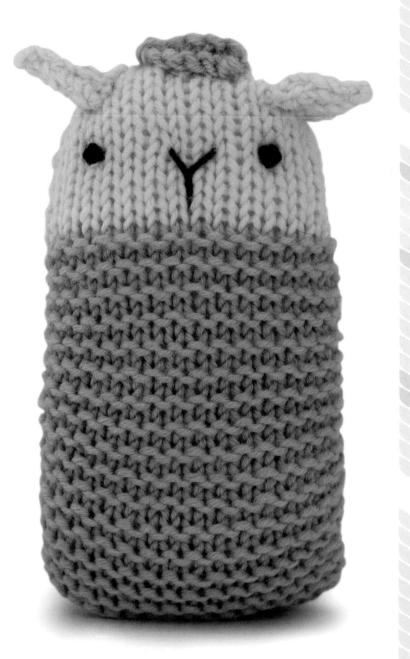

Sleepy kitten

 you will need

size
Approximately 14.5 × 6.5cm
(6 × 2½in)

materials
Sublime Baby Cashmere
Merino Silk DK 50g in
A: Splash (124) × 1
B: Muffin (278) × 1
1 pair of 3.25mm (UK10/
US3) needles
Large-eyed needle
Short length of dark grey
4-ply yarn or dark grey
embroidery thread
Toy filling
Water-soluble pen
Spray bottle (optional)

tension
22sts and 28 rows to 10cm
(4in) over st st on 3.25mm
(UK10/US3) needles

how to make

The body and head are knitted
together working from the base
to the top of the head.

Body and head (Make 2)
Cast on 18sts in yarn A.
K 34 rows.
Break yarn A and join yarn B.
Work 12 rows in st st.
Row 47: K8, cast off 2sts, k to end.
Row 48: P8, turn and work on these
8sts only, leaving rem sts on needle.
Row 49: K1, k2tog, k to end. (7sts)
Row 50: P.
Rep last 2 rows × 2. (5sts)
Row 55: K1, k2tog, k2. (4sts)
Row 56: [P2tog] × 2. (2sts)
Row 57: K2tog. (1st)
Break yarn and pull through rem st.
Rejoin yarn to rem sts on WS of work.
Row 58: P.
Row 59: K to last 3sts, ssk, k1. (7sts)
Row 60: P.
Rep last 2 rows × 2. (5sts)
Row 65: K2, ssk, k1. (4sts)
Row 66: [P2tog] × 2. (2sts)
Row 67: Ssk. (1st)
Break yarn and pull through rem st.

Making up
Join the side seams using mattress
stitch (see p.240) and matching yarns.
Turn the kitten inside out and
oversew around the ears. Turn the
kitten RS out again. Make sure all
yarn tails are secure and on the
inside of your toy. Stuff with toy
filling. Sew the lower edge closed.
Using the photograph as a guide,
draw on the kitten's features using
the water-soluble pen. Embroider
the features in backstitch using the
dark grey yarn or embroidery thread
and a large-eyed needle. Spray the
toy lightly with water to remove the
pen marks and leave to dry.

The body and head
are knitted as one piece
starting with yarn A
in garter stitch, then
switching to yarn B
in stocking stitch.

❧ you will need

size
Approximately 35cm (14in) standing

materials
Rowan Cocoon 100g in
A: Frost (806) × 2
B: Misty blue (827) × 1
Scraps of DK yarn in light brown (for the nose) and black and white (for the eyes)
1 pair of 5mm (UK6/US8) needles
1 spare needle of the same size
1 pair of 2.75mm (UK12/US2) needles
Oatmeal-coloured sewing thread
Large-eyed needle
Toy filling

tension
Tension is not critical, but tighter knitting gives the best results when stuffing

special abbreviation
G&T (gather and tie): Thread yarn end on a sewing needle, thread through remaining stitches on knitting needle, gather them up and tie off tight

Classic teddy bear

ALTHOUGH HE'S QUICK TO MAKE, this perfect teddy bear will be cherished forever. Make sure to stuff him firmly so that he is round and cuddly. We've chosen a chunky weight, merino wool natural-blend yarn, but any chunky-weight yarn in the fibre of your choice may be substituted. Choose a different colour for your bear or his waistcoat if you wish.

how to make

Head
Using 5mm (UK6/US8) needles and yarn A, cast on 10sts.
Row 1: K. (10sts)
Row 2: [Kfb] × 10. (20sts)
Rows 3–4: K.
Row 5: [Kfb, k1] × 10. (30sts)
Rows 6–7: K.
Row 8: [Kfb, k2] × 10. (40sts)
Rows 9–10: K.
Row 11: [Kfb, k3] × 10. (50sts)
K 10 rows.
Next row: [K2tog, k3] × 10. (40sts)
K 2 rows.
Next row: [K2tog, k2] × 10. (30sts)
K 2 rows.
Next row: [K2tog, k1] × 10. (20sts)
Continue for muzzle:
P 1 row.
K 1 row.
P 1 row.
Next row: [K2tog] × 2, k12, [skpo] × 2. (16sts)
P 1 row.
Next row: [K2tog] × 2, k8, [skpo] × 2. (12sts)
P 1 row
Cast off for nose end.

Make up
Gather your cast on edge at back of head and tie off tight. Join head seam together from nose tip to back of head, leaving a gap underneath for the filling. Stuff head and nose tip firmly, sew the gap closed.

Ears (Make 2)
Using 5mm (UK6/US8) needles and yarn A, cast on 6sts.
Row 1: [Kfb] × 6. (12sts)
K 5 rows
Next row: [Kfb, k2] × 4. (16sts)
K 1 row.
Next row: [K2tog, k2] × 4. (12sts)
K 5 rows
Next row: [K2tog] × 6. (6sts)
G&T tight.

Make up
Gather up your cast on edge and fold to meet the cast off edge. Join bottom seam with gathering stitches to curl the ear.

Body
Using 5mm (UK6/US8) needles and yarn A, cast on 25sts for base.
Row 1: K. (25sts)
Row 2: [Kfb] × 25. (50sts)
K until work measures 8cm (3in) from base.
Next row: [K2tog, k3] ×10. (40sts)
K 8 rows.
Next row: [K2tog, k2] × 10. (30sts)
K until work measures 16cm (6¼in) from base.
Next row: K6, [k2tog] × 2, k10, [k2tog] × 2, k6. (26sts)
K 1 row.
Cast off for neck edge.

Make up
Sew back seam together to base. Place seam in middle of back and close base seam across from side to side. Stuff firmly leaving neck edge open.

Arms (Make 2)
Using 5mm (UK6/US8) needles and yarn A, cast on 4sts.
Row 1: K. (4sts)
Row 2: Kfb, k to last stitch, kfb. (6sts)
Rep rows 1 and 2 until there are 18sts on the needle.
Next row: K. (18sts) This is the armpit.
Next row: K2tog, k14, k2tog. (16sts)
K 29 rows
Next row: [K2tog] × 8. (8sts)
G&T tight for paw end.

Make up
Join seam from paw up to armpit leaving top of arm open. Stuff firmly.

Legs (Make 2)

Using 5mm (UK6/US8) needles and yarn A, cast on 20sts.
K 2 rows.
Next row: [Kfb] × 2, k6, [kfb] × 4, k6, [kfb] × 2. (28sts)
K 1 row.
Next row: [K1, kfb] × 2, k6, [k1, kfb] × 4, k6, [kfb, k1] × 2. (36sts)
K 10 rows.
Next row: K6, [k2tog] × 12, k6. (24sts)
K 1 row.
Next row: K6, [k2tog] × 6, k6. (18sts)
K 12 rows.
Cast off for top of leg.

Make up

Join seam from top to sole leaving top of leg open. Stuff feet firmly but do not put any filling in the leg sections so that they are floppy.

Waistcoat

Using 5mm (UK6/US8) needles and yarn B, cast on 64sts.
K 15 rows.
Next row you will divide for armholes and will require a spare knitting needle: K13, k2tog. (14sts)
Turn and work on these 14sts only, using the spare needle.
K2tog, k12. (13sts)
Next row: K11, k2tog. (12sts)
K 2 rows.
Dec for front edge as follows:
K10, k2tog. (11sts)
K 2 rows.
Next row: K2tog, k9. (10sts)
K 2 rows.
Next row: K8, k2tog. (9sts)
K 2 rows.
Next row: K2tog, k7. (8sts)
K 2 rows.
Next row: K6, k2tog. (7sts)
K 2 rows.
Next row: K2tog, k5. (6sts)
K 4 rows and cast off for shoulder seam.

Rejoin yarn to remaining stitches.
K2tog, k30, k2tog. (32sts)
Turn and work on these sts only,
using the spare needle.
Next row: K2tog, k28, k2tog. (30sts)
Next row: K2tog, k26, k2tog. (28sts)
Next row: K2tog, k24, k2tog. (26sts)
Next row: K2tog, k22, k2tog. (24sts)
K 14 rows.
Next row: K5, k2tog, k10, k2tog, k5.
(22sts)
K 2 rows.
Next row: K4, k2tog, k10, k2tog, k4.
(20sts)
K 2 rows.
Cast off for shoulder seam.
Rejoin yarn to remaining stitches.
K2tog, k13. (14sts)
Next row: K12, k2tog. (13sts)
Next row: K2tog, k11. (12sts)
K 2 rows.
Dec for front edge as follows:
K2tog, k10. (11sts)
K 2 rows.
Next row: K9, k2tog. (10sts)
K 2 rows.
Next row: K2tog, k8. (9sts)
K 2 rows.
Next row: K7, k2tog. (8sts)
K 2 rows.
Next row: K2tog, k6. (7sts)
K 2 rows.
Next row: K5, k2tog. (6sts)
K 4 rows and cast off for shoulder
seam.

Make up
Sew front two sections to back
section at the shoulder and weave
in loose yarn ends (see p.242).

Nose
Using 2.75mm (UK12/US2) needles
and light brown DK scrap yarn, cast
on 7sts.
Row 1: K2tog, k3, skpo. (5sts)
P 1 row.
Next row: K2tog, k1, skpo. (3sts)

P 1 row.
Next row: K2tog, k1. (2sts)
Next row: P2tog. (1st)
Tie off.

Making up
Sew ears curved to top of head.
Position nose to cover top of nose
muzzle seam, sew around nose
edge neatly.

Make the eyes on the 2nd knit row
above the muzzle, using black yarn to
work small circles of chain stitches

spiralling in to centres. Use a scrap of
white yarn to work a highlighting stitch.

Place head on top of body and sew
around neck edge to secure it. Sew
arms to sides of top of arm at bear's
shoulder. Sew legs to bear's bottom
covering the base seam.

Position the nose so that it covers
the top of the muzzle seam. Neatly
sew it in place with the sewing thread.

Stitch the ears to the head making
sure they sit evenly on either side. Use
the main photograph as your guide.

Sew the arms to the top of the sides
of the bear's body. Make sure they are
securely attached and won't come off.

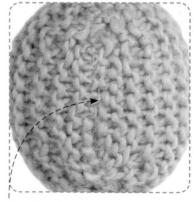

Neatly join the seam on the
bottom of each foot so that the
seam sits flat and is almost invisible.

you will need

size
Each block is 7cm (2¾in) square

materials
Debbie Bliss Baby Cashmerino
DK 50g in
Block 1
A: Sky (032) × 1
B: Apple (002) × 1
C: Ecru (101) × 1
Block 2
D: Royal (070) × 1
E: Coral (050) × 1
F: Aqua blue (031) × 1
Block 3
G: Kingfisher (072) × 1

H: Primrose (001) × 1
J: Hot pink (060) × 1
1 pair of 3.25mm (UK10/US3)
needles
Large-eyed needle
3 × 6.5cm (2½in) cubes of
upholstery foam (available from
upholstery supply stores and some
craft and haberdashery stores)
Serrated knife (if cutting the blocks
of foam yourself)

tension
Tension is not critical for
this project

Smooth the knitting over
each foam block and match up
the corners exactly for a neat
finish. Use mattress stitch (see
p.240) to close up the cubes
and secure the foam inside.

Building blocks

THESE BLOCKS ARE A GREAT PROJECT if you have scraps of DK-weight yarn you want to use up. All you need are three different-coloured yarns to make one block. Each block is made from six panels using different stitches, so it's also a fantastic project for new knitters wanting to try out an assortment of different stitches.

❧ how to make

Garter stitch panel
Make one in each of the following shades: A, D, and G.
Cast on 16sts.
K 28 rows. Cast off.

Split seed stitch panel
Make one in each of the following shades: B, F, and H.
Cast on 17sts.
Work 2 rows in st st beg with a k row
Next row: P1, [k3, p1] to end.
Work 3 rows in st st beg with a p row.
Next row: K2, p1, [k3, p1] to last 2sts, k2.
Work 3 rows in st st beg with a p row.
Rep last 8 rows once more.
Next row: P1, [k3, p1] to end.
Next row: P. Cast off.

Woven stitch panel
Make one in each of the following shades: B, E, and J.
Cast on 16sts.
Work 2 rows in st st beg with a k row.
Next row: K1, [p2, k2] to last 3sts, p2, k1.
Next row: P1, [k2, p2] to last 3sts, k2, p1.
Work 2 rows in st st beg with a k row.
Next row: P1, [k2, p2] to last 3sts, k2, p1.

Next row: K1, [p2, k2] to last 3sts, p2, k1.
Work 2 rows in st st beg with a k row.
Rep last 8 rows once more.
Next row: K1, [p2, k2] to last 3sts, p2, k1.
Next row: P1, [k2, p2] to last 3sts, k2, p1.
Work 2 rows in st st beg with a k row.
Cast off.

Garter stitch stripe panel
Make one in each of the following shades: C, E, and J.
Cast on 16sts.
Work 2 rows in st st beg with a k row.
K 2 rows.
Rep last 4 rows × 4.
Work 2 rows in st st beg with a k row.
Cast off.

Lattice stitch panel
Make one in each of the following shades: C, F, and H.
Cast on 17sts.
Row 1: K5, p1, k5, p1, k5.
Next row: P4, k1, p1, k1, p3, k1, p1, k1, p4.
Next row: K3, p1, k3, p1, k1, p1, k3, p1, k3.
Next row: P2, k1, [p5, k1] × 2, p2.
Next row: K3, p1, k3, p1, k1, p1, k3,

p1, k3.
Next row: P4, k1, p1, k1, p3, k1, p1, k1, p4.
Rep last 6 rows × 3. Cast off.

Double moss stitch panel
Make one in each of the following shades: A, D, and G.
Cast on 17sts.
Row 1: K1, [p1, k1] to end.
Next row: P1, [k1, p1] to end.
Next row: P1, [k1, p1] to end.
Next row: K1, [p1, k1] to end.
Rep last 4 rows × 4.
Next row: K1, [p1, k1] to end.
Next row: P1, [k1, p1] to end.
Cast off.

Making up
Assemble the blocks – the two panels of the same colour should lie opposite each other on the finished block. Join the seams using mattress stitch (see p.240) and a large-eyed needle. Leave one seam open.

Cut the foam to size, if necessary, with a serrated knife. Insert the foam block into each knitted case. Pull the case over the foam block and match up the corners neatly. Close the final seam using mattress stitch.

To make *a newborn set*

see pages 26–29, 180–181, and 194–195

Cheeky monkey

KNITTED ON A PAIR OF NEEDLES INSTEAD OF IN THE ROUND, this monkey is easy, even for a beginner. The monkey is worked on smaller than normal needles to make a firm fabric. When stuffing the toy, take care not to stretch the knitting as this will give it an odd shape. Make your monkey appealing by giving him a smiley mouth and friendly, alert eyes.

🌿 you will need

size
Approximately 35 × 12.5cm
(14 × 5in)

materials
King Cole Merino Blend
DK 50g in
A: Sky (05) × 2
B: Oatmeal (41) × 1
1 pair of 3mm (UK11/USn/a)
needles
6-strand embroidery thread
in black and white
Toy filling
Blunt-ended needle
Large-eyed needle

tension
28sts and 33 rows to 10cm
(4in) over st st on 3mm
(UK11/USn/a) needles, or
as near to this as you can
achieve. Tension is not critical
on this project.

🌿 how to make

Body and head
The body and head are worked in one piece, starting at the lower end of the body.
Using yarn A, cast on 20sts, leaving a long, loose end for back seam.
Row 1 (RS): [Kfb, k1] × 10. (30sts)
Row 2: P.
Row 3: K1, [M1, k3] × 9, M1, k2. (40sts)
Row 4: P.
Row 5: K2, [M1, k4] × 9, M1, k2. (50sts)
Cont in st st for 13 rows more, ending with RS facing for next row.
Cont in st st throughout as follows:
Next row (RS): K6, [k2tog, k10] × 3, k2tog, k6. (46sts)
P 1 row.
Next row: K1, [k2tog, k4] × 7, k2tog, k1. (38sts)
P 1 row.
Next row: K3, [k2tog, k8] × 3, k2tog, k3. (34sts)
P 1 row.
Next row: K4, [k2tog, k3] × 6. (28sts)
Work 9 rows without shaping, ending with RS facing for next row.

Shape shoulders
Next row (RS): K6, k2tog, k12, k2tog, k6. (26sts)

P 1 row.
Next row: K5, sk2p, k10, sk2p, k5. (22sts)
P 1 row.
Next row: K4, sk2p, k8, sk2p, k4. (18sts)
P 1 row.

Head
Next row (RS): K2, [kfb, k1] × 8. (26sts)
P 1 row.
Next row: K2, [M1, k3] × 8. (34sts)
P 1 row.
Next row: K4, [M1, k5] × 6. (40sts)
Work 17 rows without shaping, ending with RS facing for next row.
Next row: K2, [k2tog, k3] × 7, k2tog, k1. (32sts)
P 1 row.
Next row: K1, [k2tog, k2] × 7, k2tog, k1. (24sts)
P 1 row.
Next row: [K2tog, k1] × 8. (16sts)
P 1 row.
Next row: [K2tog] × 8. (8sts)
Next row: [P2tog] × 4. (4sts)
Cut off yarn, leaving a long, loose yarn tail. Thread end onto a blunt-ended yarn needle and pass needle through 4 rem sts as they are dropped from needle. Pull yarn to gather stitches and secure with a few stitches.

Knit the body starting at the base of the body, cast on loosely and knit the fabric as instructed. Shape the knitting with kfb and then M1 increases (see pp.219–221).

Position the top of the arms just below the start of the shoulder shape. Ensure that the diagonal top edge is the correct way up so the arm seam faces the body.

Stuff the muzzle firmly and evenly with toy filling. Sew on the muzzle, making tiny stitches that will not be obvious against the light blue yarn of the head.

Legs (Make 2)

Each leg is started at the foot end. Using yarn B, cast on 6sts using a single cast on method and leaving a long, loose yarn tail.
Row 1 (RS): [Kfb] × 5, k1. (11sts)
Row 2: P.
Row 3: K1, [M1, k1] × 10. (21sts)
Beg with a p row, work 9 rows in st st, ending with RS facing for next row.
Row 13 (RS): K2, [k2tog, k3] × 3, k2tog, k2. (17sts)
Row 14: P.
Cut off yarn B.
Cont in st st in yarn A throughout as follows:
Work 10 rows without shaping, ending with RS facing for next row.
Next row (RS): K4, k2tog, k6, k2tog, k3. (15sts)
Work 15 rows without shaping.
Next row (RS): K3, [k2tog, k2] × 2, k2tog, k2. (12sts)**
Work 11 rows without shaping.
Cast off knitwise.

Arms (Make 2)

Each arm is started at the hand end.
Work as for Legs to **.
Work 7 rows without shaping.

Cast off 2sts at beg of next 4 rows.
Cast off rem 4sts, leaving a long, loose yarn tail for sewing arm to body.

Muzzle

Using yarn B, cast on 6sts, using a single cast on method and leaving a long, loose yarn tail.
Row 1 (RS): [Kfb] × 5, k1. (11sts)
Row 2: P.
Row 3: K1, [M1, k1] × 10. (21sts)
Row 4: P.
Row 5: K1, [M1, k2] × 10. (31sts)
Beg with a p row, work 5 rows in st st.
Cast off knitwise, leaving a long, loose yarn tail for sewing muzzle to body.

Ears (Make 2)

Using yarn B, cast on 3sts.
Row 1 (WS): [Kfb] × 2, k1. (5sts)
Please note: Work the remaining increases as yarnovers (see pp.222–224), ensuring that each yarnover is crossed when it is knit in the following row to close the hole by knitting it through the back of the loop (see p.218).
Row 2 (RS): [K1, yrn] × 4, k1. (9sts)
Row 3: K to end, knitting each yrn through back loop.

Row 4: [K2, yrn] × 4, k1. (13sts)
Row 5: Rep row 3.
Row 6: K.
K 2 rows.
Cast off loosely knitwise, leaving a long, loose yarn tail for gathering ear into cupped shape and sewing to head.

Tail

Using yarn B, cast on 3sts, leaving a long, loose yarn tail for sewing tail to body.
Work in g st until tail is a little longer than leg (or desired length).
Next row: Sk2p, then fasten off.
Tail will swirl naturally – do not press out this swirl.

Making up
Legs

Using the long yarn tail, weave in and out of the cast on stitches using mattress stitch (see p.240), then pull to gather. Sew the leg seam, stuffing as you proceed. Pinch the end of each leg together, with the seam at the centre of the back of each leg, and sew the end closed with overcast stitches. Repeat for the second leg.

Body and head

Starting at the cast on edge and using mattress stitch, sew 2.5cm (1in) of the back seam on the body. Position cast off edge of legs inside the body in the lower body seam. Next, sew the lower body seam with overcast stitches, catching in the legs. Cont the back body seam, stuffing the body evenly with toy filling. Cont the seam up the back of the head. Make sure the head is packed with filling before completing the seam. Secure the yarn with two or three small stitches.

Arms

Prepare the arms in the same way as for Legs, but do not sew the tops of the arms closed. Using the photograph as a guide, position the top of the arm just below the beginning of the shoulder shaping and pin in place. Keep the arm ends open so that they meet the body in a circle and slant downwards. Sew the arms in place, turning the edges of the arm inside as you stitch. Remove the pins as you stitch.

Muzzle

Using the yarn tail, stitch in and out of the cast on stitches and pull to gather. Sew the muzzle seam using mattress stitch, starting at the cast on edge. Trim the seam yarn to 5cm (2in) long and place inside the muzzle. Fill the muzzle with toy filling. Pin the muzzle to the head, forming an oval shape covering about 10 stitches across the face and about 12 rows. Sew the muzzle in place with short overcast stitches.

Ears

Darn in the end. Make widely spaced overcast stitches along the straight edge of each ear. Gather these stitches to form the ear into a cup shape. Using the gathering yarn, sew the ears to the sides of the head. Pull the stitches tight so they disappear. Follow the photograph, below, as a guide.

Tail

Sew the tail at the base of the monkey's back using the long yarn tail. Darn in the other yarn tail at the cast off edge of the monkey's tail.

Face

Use a large-eyed needle and all six strands of the embroidery thread for the facial features. Use the photograph (right) as a guide. Work the features carefully, redoing them if necessary. The curve of the eyebrows will give your monkey its expression. To personalize your toy, alter the position and size of the eyes, and the shape of the mouth and eyebrows. Even changing the ear positions can give him a unique look.

Embroider the facial features using embroidery thread, or try off-cuts of black and white DK yarn if you have them.

Gather the stitches along the straight edge of the ear to form a cup. Use the gathering yarn to sew the ears to the sides of the head.

Attach the tail using a large-eyed needle. Knot the end and take the needle through the underside of the tail so it does not show.

Jumping bunnies

MAKING THESE IRREGULARLY SHAPED RABBITS is a great way to hone your increasing and decreasing skills. We've used simple embroidery to create the facial features and mattress stitch for an almost seamless back. A simple, neat pom-pom makes a perfect fluffy tail. You could try adding a heavy weight inside the bottom of one rabbit to use it as a door stop.

🌿 you will need

size
12.5cm (5in) tall

materials
Rowan Wool Cotton 50g in
Lavender bunny
A: Frozen (977) × 1
B: Antique white (900) × 1
Blue bunny
C: Cypress (968) × 1
D: Clear (941) × 1
Pink bunny
E: Flower (943) × 1
F: Tender (951) × 1
1 pair of 3mm (UK11/USn/a)
needles
Stitch marker
Toy filling
Dried chickpeas (for weight)
Large-eyed needle
Short length of yarn or
embroidery thread in
contrasting colours for
embroidering the face

tension
30sts and 37 rows to 10cm
(4in) over st st on 3mm
(UK11/USn/a) needles

🌿 how to make

Body
Cast on 16sts in yarn A (C:E), placing marker at centre of cast on edge.
Row 1: Inc into every st to end. (32sts)
Row 2 and all foll alt rows: P.
Row 3: [K1, inc in next st] to end. (48sts)
Row 5: [K2, inc in next st] × 3, k to last 7sts, [inc in next st, k2] × 2, inc in last st. (54sts)
Row 7: K.
Row 9: [K3, inc in next st] × 3, [k2, inc in next st] to last 12sts, [inc in next st, k3] to end. (70sts)
Row 11: K.
Row 13: [K4, inc in next st] × 3, k to last 11sts, [inc in next st, k4] × 2, inc in last st. (76sts)
Work 13 rows without shaping.

Shape back
Row 1: [K3, k2tog] × 6, k to last 27sts, [k2tog, k3] × 5, k2tog. (64sts)
Work 3 rows without shaping.
Row 5: [K2, k2tog] × 6, k to last 22sts, [k2tog, k2] × 5, k2tog. (52sts)
Next and all foll alt rows: P.
Row 7: [K1, k2tog] × 4, k to last 11sts, [k2tog, k1] × 3, k2tog. (44sts)
Row 9: K12, k2tog, k2, k2tog, k8, k2tog, k2, k2tog, k to end. (40sts)
Row 11: K1, k2tog, k to last 3sts, k2tog, k1. (38sts)
Row 13: K10, k2tog, k2, k2tog, k6, k2tog, k2, k2tog, k to end. (34sts)
Row 15: K1, k2tog, k to last 3sts, k2tog, k1. (32sts)
Work 7 rows without shaping.

Shape head
Row 1: [K2, k2tog] to end. (24sts)
Row 2 and all foll alt rows: P.
Row 3: [K1, k2tog] to end. (16sts)
Row 5: [K2tog] to end. (8sts)
Using a large-eyed needle, draw yarn through rem sts twice. Join row ends to form back seam, using mattress stitch (see p.240) and leaving bottom open. Stuff firmly with toy filling, inserting a layer of chickpeas at the

base of the bunny to provide a bit of weight. An entire filling of chickpeas would make it heavy and lumpy, but combining them with a light filling works well. Line up back seam with marker at bunny's front and squash flat. Oversew this seam together.

Tail

Make a 3cm (1¼in) pom-pom (see p.247) from yarn B (D:E), or a mix of colours. Securely sew the pom-pom to the back of the bunny.

Spots (Make 3)

Using yarn B (D:E), cast on 3sts.
Row 1: K.
Row 2: Inc in first st, p1, inc in last st. (5sts)
Row 3: K.
Row 4: P.
Row 5: K.

Row 6: P2tog, p1, p2tog. (3sts)
Row 7: K.
Cast off, leaving a long yarn tail. Arrange spots randomly on bunny and, using long yarn tail, oversew in place (see below, left).

Feet (Make 2)

Using yarn A (C:E), cast on 6sts.
Row 1: K.
Row 2: P.
Rep last 2 rows five times more.
Cast off.
With RS facing, oversew cast on and cast off edges together. This seam forms the back of the foot. Using the photographs as a guide, pin in place and oversew to underside of body.

Ears (Make 2)

Using yarn A (C:E), cast on 6sts and work 10 rows st st.

Next row (RS): K1, skpo, k2tog, k1. (4sts)
Next row: P.
Change to yarn B (D:F).
Next row: K2, M1, k2. (5sts)
Beginning with a p row, work 9 rows st st.
Cast off.
Fold ear piece in half to match cast on to cast off edge. Join row ends and stitch in position on the top of the head. If you wish, catch one or both ears down with a single stitch to affix to the bunny's head.

Using a strand of yarn or embroidery thread in a contrasting colour, embroider the eyes and nose in satin stitch (see p.244).

Attach the bunny's spots by oversewing in place. You can place the spots where ever you like, or leave them off altogether; it's up to you.

Oversew the feet to the underside of the bunny. Make sure the seam is at the back of the foot, where it attaches to the underside.

The bunny's face can wear any expression: use satin stitch, shown on p.244, to create the expression. The ears can be left up or sewn down.

top tip

When working
with pins,
always double-
check they
have all been
removed.

A pom-pom is quick to make (see p.247). When tying yarn around the centre of it, leave two long ends: use these to sew it in place.

T-rex toy

FAR FROM BEING SCARY, this lovable T-rex makes a great play-mate. Knitted using a soft, washable, bamboo cotton yarn, it is both tough and cuddly. As with all toys, make sure the toy filling you select is also washable. There are a variety of toy fillings available, so choose one you are comfortable using depending on its fibre content and care requirements.

❧ how to make

Please note: When casting off 1 stitch will be left on the RH needle that isn't counted in the number of stitches in the instructions that follow.

Head and body

(Worked from nose, through head and down body to tail)
Using yarn A, cast on 7sts using the cable cast on method, working between stitches.
Row 1: Inc in every st. (14sts)
P 1 row.
Next row: K1, M1, [k2, M1] × 6, k1. (21sts)
P 1 row.
Next row: K1, M1, [k3, M1] × 6, k2. (28sts)
Beg with a p row, work 3 rows in st st.
Next row: K7, M1, k14, M1, k7. (30sts)

Beg with a p row, work 5 rows in st st.
Next row: K8, M1, k1, M1, k12, M1, k1, M1, k8. (34sts)
P 1 row.
Next row: K11, M1, k1, M1, k10, M1, k1, M1, k11. (38sts)
P 1 row.
Next row: K14, M1, k10, M1, k14. (40sts)
P 1 row.

Shape the head

Commence short row knitting as follows:
Next row: K38, turn.
Next row: Yb, s1p, yfwd, p35, turn.
Next row: Yfwd, s1p, yb, k33, turn.
Next row: Yb, s1p, yfwd, p31, turn.
Next row: Yfwd, s1p, yb, k29, turn.
Next row: Yb, s1p, yfwd, p27, turn.
Next row: Yfwd, s1p, yb, k25, turn.
Next row: Yb, s1p, yfwd, p23, turn.
Next row: Yfwd, s1p, yb, k21, turn.
Next row: Yb, s1p, yfwd, p19, turn.
Next row: Yfwd, s1p, yb, k17, turn.
Next row: Yb, s1p, yfwd, p15, turn.
Next row: Yfwd, s1p, yb, k15, turn.
On the following rows, when a st that has been slipped on a previous row is about to be worked: with the RH needle, pick up the wrapped strand around the slipped st on the

LH needle and place it on the LH needle in front of all the sts, k or p it tog with the slipped st tbl.
Next row: Yb, s1p, yfwd, p17, turn.
Next row: Yfwd, s1p, yb, k19, turn.
Next row: Yb, s1p, yfwd, p21, turn.
Next row: Yfwd, s1p, yb, k23, turn.
Next row: Yb, s1p, yfwd, p25, turn.
Next row: Yfwd, s1p, yb, k27, turn.
Next row: Yb, s1p, yfwd, p29, turn.
Next row: Yfwd, s1p, yb, k31, turn.
Next row: Yb, s1p, yfwd, p33, turn.
Next row: Yfwd, s1p, yb, k35, turn.
Next row: P to end.
Next row: K1, [skpo, k2] × 5, [k2tog, k2] × 4, k2tog, k1. (30sts)
P 1 row.
Next row: K28, turn.
Next row: Yb, s1p, yfwd, p25, turn.
Next row: Yfwd, s1p, yb, k23, turn.
Next row: Yb, s1p, yfwd, p21, turn.
Next row: Yfwd, s1p, yb, k19, turn.
Next row: Yb, s1p, yfwd, p17, turn.
Next row: Yfwd, s1p, yb, k15, turn.
Next row: Yb, s1p, yfwd, p13, turn.
Next row: Yfwd, s1p, yb, k11, turn.
Next row: Yb, s1p, yfwd, p to end.
Place markers at each end of last row.

Body

Beg with a k row, work 8 rows in st st.
Next row: [K1, M1 × 2, k6, M1 × 2, k1,

Attach the arms to either side of the body, making sure they are equally placed. Place the edge with the seam facing downwards on both sides.

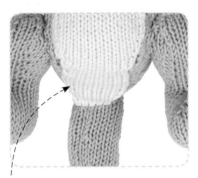

Sew the tummy panel to the sides of the body, then around the cast off edges of the lower body and to the base of the tail.

The head is shaped using short rows and decreases to give smooth curves to both the crown and jaw.

M1 × 2, k6, M1 × 2, k1] × 2. (38sts)
Beg with a p row, work 7 rows in st st.
Next row: [K4, M1] × 3, k7, M1, k7, [M1, k4] × 3. (45sts)
Beg with a p row, work 17 rows in st st.

Shape the tail

Next row: K1, [skpo, k2] × 3, k8, [M1, k1] × 4, k7, [k2, k2tog] × 3, k1. (43sts)
P 1 row.
Next row: K1, [skpo, k2] × 3, k7, [M1, k1] × 4, k6, [k2, k2tog] × 3, k1. (41sts)
P 1 row.
Next row: K1, [skpo, k2] × 3, k6, [M1, k1] × 4, k5, [k2, k2tog] × 3, k1. (39sts)
P 1 row.

Divide for tail

Next row: Cast off 12sts, k14, cast off 12sts to end.
Break yarn.
With WS facing, rejoin yarn to rem 15sts and cont as follows:
Next row: Cast on 3sts, p to end. (18sts)
Next row: Cast on 3sts, k to end. (21sts)
Beg with a p row, work 13 rows in st st.
Next row: K1, skpo, k to last 3sts, k2tog, k1.
Beg with a p row, work 3 rows in st st.
Rep the last 4 rows × 3. (13sts)
Next row: K1, *k2tog, rep from * to end. (7sts)
P 1 row.
Next row: K1, *k2tog, rep from * to end. (4sts)
Break off yarn leaving a long tail and draw this through rem sts twice, pull up tightly.

Tummy panel

Using yarn B, cast on 7sts using the cable cast on method, working between stitches.
Beg with a k row, work 4 rows in st st.
Inc 1st at each end of next row. (9sts)

Beg with a p row, work 11 rows in st st.
Place markers at each end of last row.
Beg with a k row, work 2 rows in st st.
Inc 1st at each end of next row.
Beg with a p row, work 3 rows in st st.
Rep the last 4 rows × 2. (15sts)
Beg with a k row, work 12 rows in st st.
Dec 1st at each end of next row.
Beg with a p row, work 5 rows in st st.
Rep the last 6 rows × 1. (11sts)
Dec 1st at each end of next and every foll alt row until 3sts rem.
P 1 row.
Next row: Skpo, slip st just made back onto the LH needle and k2tog.
Break yarn, thread through rem st, pull up tightly and fasten off.

Legs (Make 2)

Using yarn A cast on 32sts using the cable cast on method.
Beg with a k row, work 2 rows in st st.
Next row: K1, [inc in next st, k13, inc in next st] × 2, k1. (36sts)
P 1 row.
Next row: [K1, inc in next st, k14, inc in next st, k1] × 2. (40sts)
Beg with a p row, work 5 rows in st st.
Next row: [K1, skpo, k14, k2tog, k1] × 2. (36sts)
P 1 row.
Next row: K1, [skpo, k13, k2tog] × 2, k1. (32sts)
P 1 row.
Next row: K8, cast off 16sts, k7.
Next row: P across all 16sts.
Beg with a k row, work 2 rows in st st.
Next row: [K1, inc in next st, k4, inc in next st, k1] × 2. (20sts)
P 1 row.
Next row: [K1, inc in next st, k6, inc in next st, k1] × 2. (24sts)
P 1 row.
Next row: [K1, inc in next st, k8, inc in next st, k1] × 2. (28sts)
P 1 row.
Next row: [K1, inc in next st, k10, inc

in next st, k1] × 2. (32sts)
Beg with a p row, work 3 rows in st st.
Next row: [K1, skpo, k10, k2tog, k1]
× 2. (28sts)
P 1 row.
Next row: [K1, skpo, k8, k2tog, k1]
× 2. (24sts)
P 1 row.
Next row: (K1, skpo, k6, k2tog, k1)
× 2. (20sts)
P 1 row.
Cast off.

Arms (Make 2)

Using yarn A cast on 9sts using the
cable cast on method.
Beg with a k row, work 10 rows in st st.
Next row: K1, [M1, k1] to end. (17sts)
P 1 row.
Next row: Inc in first st, k1, turn.
P 1 row on these 3sts only.

Next row: Skpo, slip st just made
back onto the LH needle and k2tog.
Break yarn, thread through rem st,
pull up tightly and fasten off.
**With RS facing, rejoin yarn to rem
sts and cont as follows:
Next row: K3, turn.
P 1 row on these 3sts only.
Next row: Skpo, slip st just made
back onto the LH needle and k2tog.
Break yarn, thread through rem st,
pull up tightly and fasten off. **
Rep from ** to ** × 4 (6 claws
worked altogether).

Making up
Head and body

Sew seam from cast on edge at
nose, under chin and down neck
to markers. Then sew cast on edge
nose seam. Stuff head firmly. Place

tummy panel between side edges
of body with point at neck markers.
Pin in place with markers on tummy
panel level with cast off edge of body.
Sew to body down each side of
tummy panel. Stuff the body firmly,
moulding and shaping as you go.
Next sew tail seam and stuff tail.
Sew remainder of tummy panel to
cast off edges of body and edges of
tail at underside of body.

Legs

Sew cast off edges along top of
foot together. Then sew seam from
underside of toe, along foot and up
heel and back leg to cast off edge. Stuff
firmly then close the top edges. Place
legs on each side of body in positions
as shown and sew on securely.

Arms

Fold each arm in half with WS
together and oversew around each
of the three claws and along the side
edges to join. Stuff arms firmly then
sew cast on edge to body in positions
as shown.

Features and teeth

Using two strands of black
embroidery thread work nostrils in
satin stitch (see p.244) on nose, as
shown in the photo. Then embroider
eyes in the same way, sewing a small
highlight in each eye with white
embroidery thread. Cut a strip of
white felt measuring 9cm (3½in) long
and 0.5cm (¼in) wide. Cut triangles
for teeth along one edge being
careful not to cut right through
the strip. Place the strip of teeth
on the toy and curve up ends until
you are happy with the position and
expression. Using white thread, sew
through the felt fabric to the toy,
working one small stitch on each
tooth, to hold in place.

Rattle ball

YOU DON'T NEED TO KNOW how to knit in the round to make this simple striped ball; it is knitted on straight needles and then joined together with mattress stitch. The contrasting colour stripes and rattle, sewn inside, make it of both visual and auditory interest to curious babies. Choose black and white yarns for even more contrast if you wish.

how to make

Pattern

Cast on 6sts in yarn A.
1st row: (Inc 1st) x 6. (12sts)
K 2 rows.
Next row: [K1, M1] to last st, k1. (23sts)
Next row: K.
Next row (RS): K4, [M1, k3] x 5, M1, k4. (29sts)
Next row: K.
Leave yarn A at side and join yarn B.
K 2 rows.
Next row: K4, [M1, k3] x 7, M1, k4. (37sts)
K 3 rows.
Leave yarn B at side and use yarn A.
K 2 rows.
Next row: [K3, M1] x 11, k4. (48sts)
K 3 rows.
Leave yarn A at side and use yarn B.
K 2 rows.
Next row: [K3, M1] x 15, k3. (63sts)
K 3 rows.
Leave yarn B at side and use yarn A.
K 2 rows.
Next row: K1, [k2tog, k3] x 12, k2tog. (50sts)
K 3 rows.
Leave yarn A at side and use yarn B.
K 2 rows.
Next row: [K3, k2tog] to end. (40sts)
K 3 rows.

Break yarn B and use yarn A for remainder of toy.
K 2 rows.
Next row: [K2, k2tog] to end. (30sts)
Next row: K.
Next row: [K2tog] to end. (15sts)
Next row: K.
Next row: [K2tog] x 3, sk2p, [k2tog] x 3. (7sts)
Break yarn, thread it through rem sts and secure.

Making up

Prepare the rattle by wrapping it in a layer of toy filling about 2cm (¾in) thick, and winding a length of yarn round the "parcel" to secure the rattle in the centre. This is necessary to stop the rattle working its way to the edge of the filling when it is inside the ball.

Join the side seam of the ball using mattress stitch (see p.240), leaving a gap of a few centimetres (1in) for filling. Stuff the ball firmly and insert the wrapped rattle in the centre. Close the opening using mattress stitch. Weave in any yarn ends and cut.

Wrap the rattle in a layer of filling and secure it with scrap yarn. This will prevent it from moving around.

Be sure to line up your stripes in straight rows as you stitch up the seam using mattress stitch (see p.240).

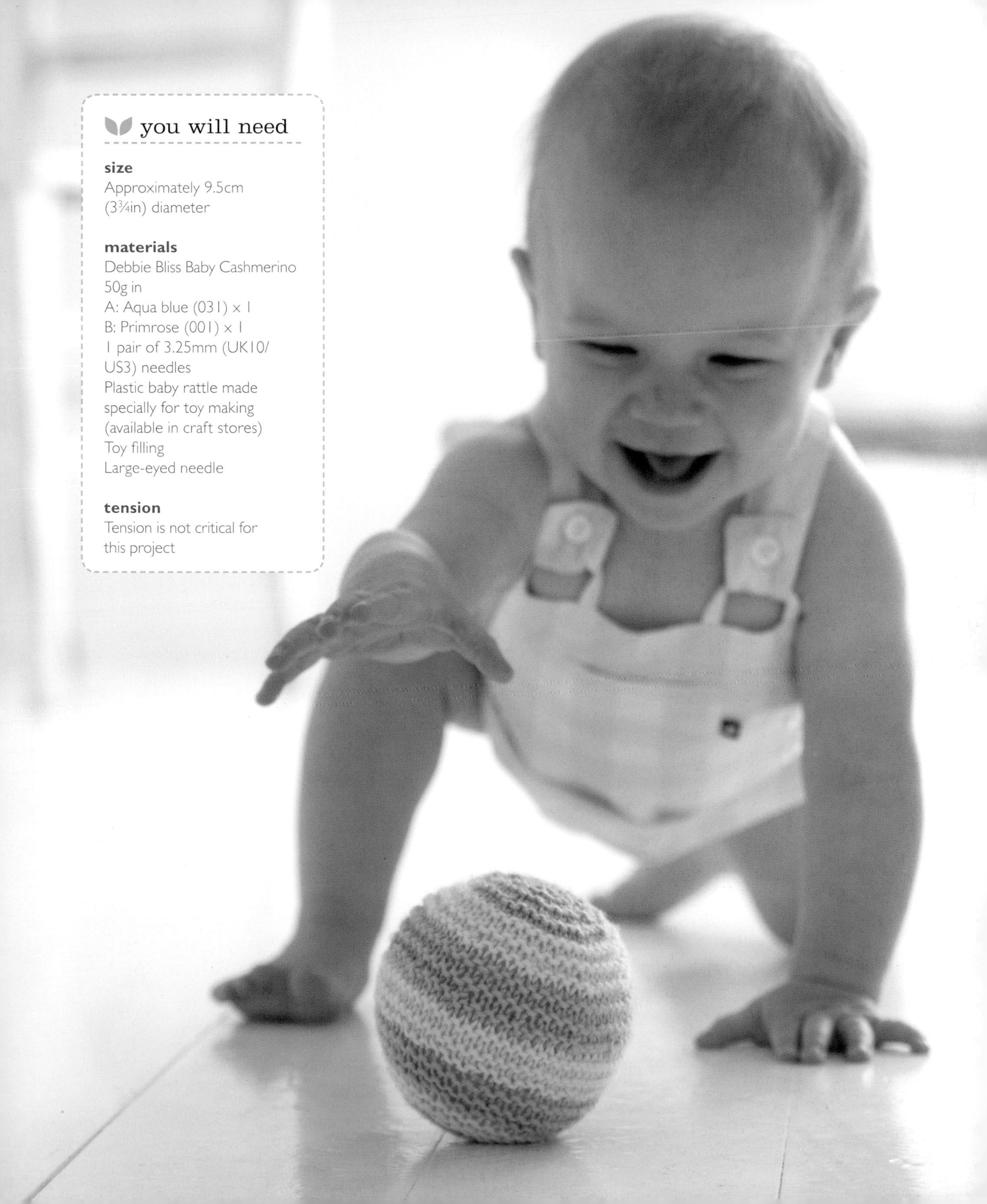

size
Approximately 9.5cm
(3¾in) diameter

materials
Debbie Bliss Baby Cashmerino
50g in
A: Aqua blue (031) × 1
B: Primrose (001) × 1
1 pair of 3.25mm (UK10/
US3) needles
Plastic baby rattle made
specially for toy making
(available in craft stores)
Toy filling
Large-eyed needle

tension
Tension is not critical for
this project

Sunny pram toy

A DOUBLE-SIDED DAY AND NIGHT pram toy will help you teach your baby about waking and sleeping. The brightly coloured day-time side has an alert face and the darker night-time side has a sleepy face. The amount of yarn balls needed is sufficient to make more than one toy, so you can change the colourways and faces to suit your own personal taste.

🌿 you will need

size
Approximately 20cm (7½in) in diameter

materials
Wendy Supreme Luxury Cotton DK 50g in
A: Seashell (1946) × 1
B: Lime (1928) × 1
C: Sunflower (1922) × 1
D: French blue (1924) × 1
E: Cream (1851) × 1
Small amounts of deep pink, white, and blue yarn for embroidery
Toy filling
1 pair of 3.25mm (UK10/US3) needles
Blunt-ended needle

tension
Tension is not critical when making this project, but work tightly to prevent the filling showing through

🌿 how to make

Centre face (Make 2)
Make 1 in yarn A and 1 in yarn B.
Cast on 10sts in yarn A (B).
K 2 rows g st.
Inc 1st at each end of the next and foll alt rows until you have 24sts.
Work 20 rows g st on these stitches.
Now dec 1st at each end of next and foll alt rows until 10sts remain.
K 2 rows and cast off.

Sun rays (Make 16)
Make 8 in yarn C and 8 in yarn D.
Cast on 8sts in yarn C (D).
K 2 rows g st.
Now inc 1st at each end of the next row and following alt rows until you have 14sts.
Work straight in g st for 10 rows.
Now dec 1st at end of the next row and foll alt rows until you have 2sts, k2tog, fasten off.

Embroider different expressions
on each side of the toy. If you'd like to be able to hang the toy, as seen opposite, securely sew a short length of ribbon to the top sun ray. Be sure it is not so long that it could become tangled and cause an injury.

Plaits
Make 2 lengths in yarn E and 1 length each in yarns A, B, C, and D.

Use two strands of the required yarn. Finger knit a chain consisting of 76 links (see below). Fasten off.

Finger knitting: Start by making a slip knot at the beginning of your yarn. Now pull the loop of the slip knot out large enough so that you can get your thumb and first finger through.

Pinch the yarn between your thumb and first finger and pull a new loop through the first loop. Pull on the new loop until the original loop is firm and neat and forms a chain. Continue to pull a new loop through the previous loop and to pull up the slack in the old loop. Continue until the chain is as long as you require. To finish, cut the yarn and pull the yarn through the last loop.

Making up

Make the rays by joining them together in pairs, one knitted in yarn C with one knitted in yarn D together. Join the sides leaving the base open. Stuff lightly. Close the bottom seam.

Arrange the sun rays, yarn C facing you, around the centre piece knitted in yarn B, WS up. Pin them in position and then when you are happy with how they look, stitch them firmly in place. Place the centre piece knitted in yarn A over the rays, RS up, and then sew in place sandwiching the rays between the two pieces. Stuff lightly to pad out before finally closing the seam.

Take the lengths of chain you have made. Plait together 1 piece each of yarn A, C, and E. Fasten off, then join into a circle, weaving in ends to give a very neat appearance. Place the circle onto the centre of the side in yarns A and C, sew in place all around the edges. Plait the remaining strips and fasten them together in the same way. Sew the plait into a circle as before and attach to the side in yarns B and D.

Embroider a happy face on one side of the centre and a sleepy face on the other side, using the photographs as a guide. (See pp.244–245 for more information on embroidery stitches.)

As with all toys, be sure to sew everything together firmly so there will be no danger of pieces coming off when the toy is played with. Always supervise your child during play.

For the nursery

Hooded blanket

GARTER STITCH AND BROKEN RIBS are used to create this pretty hooded baby blanket, which has contrast-colour edges. The pattern is completely reversible; just turn the hood over to whichever side you wish to use. Knitted in 100 per cent merino wool it's perfect for snuggling up in right before bedtime. Choose colours that will suit your special little recipient.

you will need

size
Approximately 66cm (26in) square

materials
Rico Design Essentials Soft Merino Aran 50g in
A: Curry (064) × 3
B: Light grey (020) × 4
1 pair of 5.5mm (UK5/US9) needles
2 × stitch holders

tension
16sts and 26 rows to 10cm (4in) over st st on 5.5mm (UK5/US9)

Please note: The main pattern is stretchy, so when measuring the work pull it out slightly first

how to make

Blanket
Cast on 108sts in yarn A.
K 12 rows g st.
Next row: K9, and leave sts on a stitch holder, k to last 9sts, slip these sts on a stitch holder.
Change to yarn B and proceed in patt as follows:

Row 1: *K1, p1, rep from * to end.
Row 2: K.
These 2 rows form the pattern.
Cont in patt until work measures approx. 62cm (24½in). Leave these stitches on your needle for the time being.

The contrast edging for the sides is knitted as strips and then sewn in place. Make sure to double check all pins have been removed before using the blanket.

Now return to one set of 9sts left on holders. Rejoin yarn A and work in g st until strip, when slightly stretched, fits up the side of the blanket, leave sts on holder and then do the same with the other side. Now work across 1 set of 9sts, proceed to work across stitches of main piece and then the other set of 9sts.
Continue in yarn A on these 108sts for a further 12 rows g st.
Cast off.

Hood
Cast on 4sts in yarn A.
K 2 rows.
Now Inc 1st at each end of next and foll alt rows until you have 22sts.
Now inc 1st at each end of every following 3rd row until you have 46sts.
Work 2 rows g st.
Cast off.

Making up
Lay the main blanket piece on a large, flat surface. Pin the side strips in place along each side edge of the blanket, then carefully stitch in place. Take the hood section and sew in place onto one corner of the blanket. Leave the base section open to create the hood.

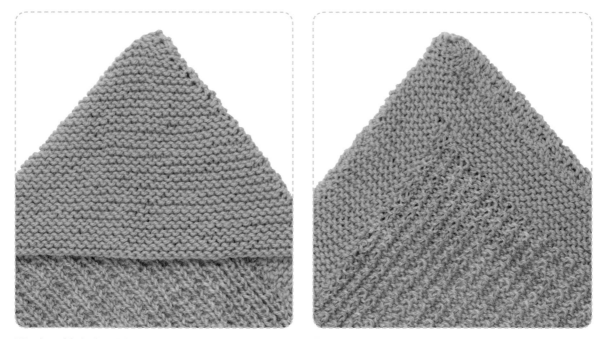

The hood is knitted in garter stitch creating a warm, stretchy, reversible fabric. Attach the hood using mattress stitch (see p.240) for an invisible, flat seam.

The reverse side can also be the right side, simply flip the hood inside out and over if you prefer to use one side as opposed to the other.

Snail cushion

THIS CHEERY PILLOW goes perfectly in a girl's bedroom. You can knit the shell and body using her favourite colours and even add a patterned ribbon around the snail's neck. Have fun giving your snail an award-winning grin by evenly working embroidery stitches in the expression of your choice. Make sure everything is securely sewn together when making up.

you will need

size
27cm (10½in) diameter shell

materials
Sublime Egyptian Cotton DK
50g in:
A: Frothy (321) × 1
B: Bud pink (323) × 2
1 pair of 4mm (UK8/US6)
needles
1 pair of 3.75mm (UK9/US5)
double-pointed needles
Toy filling
Scrap of black yarn for eyes
and mouth
Scrap of ribbon for neck

tension
22sts and 28 rows to 10cm
(4in) over st st on 4mm
(UK8/US6) needles

special abbreviations
s2kpo: s2, k1, p2sso (see
p.227)
kfbf: k into front, back, and
front of next stitch

how to make

Body
With 4mm (UK8/US6) needles and yarn A, cast on 10sts.
Row 1 (WS): K.
Rows 2 and 4: P.
Row 3: K1, kfb, k to last 2sts, kfb, k1.
Rep rows 3 and 4 until there are 30sts on the needle, finishing with a p row.
Next row: Rep row 3.
Next row: P.
Next row: K.
Next row: P.
Rep these 4 rows × 4. (38sts)
Work st st until piece measures 35cm (14in) from cast on edge, ending with a p row.

Neck and head
Row 1: K2, [skpo, k12, k2tog, k2] × 2. (34sts)
Row 2 and all even rows: P.
Row 3: K2, [s2kpo, k8, k3tog, k2] × 2. (26sts)
Row 5: K to end.
Row 7: K2 [kfbf, k8, kfbf, k2] × 2. (34sts)

Row 9: K2 [kfb, k12, kfb, k2] × 2. (38sts)
Work 13 rows st st starting and ending with a p row.
Rep rows 1–4 once more. (26sts)
Next row: K2, [s2kpo, k4, k3tog, k2] × 2. (18sts)
Next row: P.
Next row: K2tog to end. (9sts)
Thread yarn through and fasten off.

top tip

The most accurate way to evenly measure knitting is to count rows and stitches.

Antennae (Make 2)

With 3.75mm (UK9/US5) double-pointed needles and yarn A, cast on 3sts.

*K3, do not turn work, slide sts to right end of needle, pull yarn around back of sts to tighten.

Rep from * until cord measures 9cm (3½in).

Cast off.

Shell

With 4mm (UK8/US6) needles and yarn B, cast on 34sts.

Row I (RS): K to end.

Rows 2, 4, 6, and 8: P.

Row 3: K2, [p1, k3] rep to end.

Row 5: K.

Row 7: K4, [p1, k3] rep to last 2sts, p1, k1.

Rep rows 1–8 until piece measures 135cm (53in) from cast on edge.

Cast off.

Making up
Body

Fold body piece in half lengthways, RS (reverse stocking stitch) together and sew along length leaving a small gap in seam. Gather and secure at tail end. Turn through, stuff, and close gap in seam.

Shell

Fold shell piece in half lengthways, RS together and sew seam along length.

Keep the spiral straight by matching the central seam line on the tube to the central line you've drawn on the direct opposite side of the tube. This will keep your knitting from looking twisted.

Give your snail a winning smile with a few embroidery stitches and some black yarn or embroidery thread. You could also try slipping a bead on each antenna before sewing them on.

Sew seam across one end, with previous seam centralized. Turn through and stuff. Close second end in the same way as first.

Mark a central line along the top of the "tube" then roll and stitch as you go, matching the seam running the length of the tube and the central line of the roll beneath, to keep the spiral straight.

Stitch body to shell in the same way. Tie a knot in the end of each antenna and stitch to top of head. Embroider eyes and mouth, then finish with a strip of ribbon tied around the neck, securing it in place with a few stitches.

Reverse stocking stitch is used for the body and a widely spaced seed stitch for the shell. When making up the body, make sure you treat the reverse stocking stitch side as the RS of the fabric.

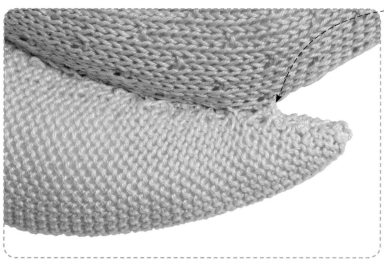

Stitch the body to the shell aligning the seam on the body to the centre of the knitting on the shell. Count the stitches on the knitting of the shell to find the exact centre.

Yacht mobile

KEEP YOUR LITTLE SEA-LOVER entertained with this yacht mobile made with garter stitch hulls in blue and red and stocking stitch sails. Remember, you should never hang a mobile above your baby's cot or leave your baby unattended around a mobile. Mobiles are not toys and should always be kept out of reach of babies and children to avoid any accidents.

🌿 you will need

size
Each yacht is approximately 7cm (2¾in) high (excluding flag)

materials
Rowan Pure Wool DK 50g in
A: Snow (012) × 1
B: Kiss (036) × 1
Rowan Cashsoft DK 50g in
C: Blue jacket (505) × 1
1 pair of 3.25mm (UK10/ US3) needles
Toy filling
A small piece of red felt
A piece of white craft foam measuring approximately 7 × 20cm (2¾ × 8in)
2 × 32cm (12½in) lengths of 14 gauge silver wire
3.5m (137in) of 3mm (⅛in) beading thread
Pale grey embroidery thread or thin yarn
Blunt-ended needle
Round nose jewellery making pliers
PVA craft glue

🌿 how to make

Make three yachts with a hull in yarn C and stripe in yarn B, and two yachts with a hull in yarn B and stripe in yarn C. Tension is not critical on this project.

Hull (Make 2 for each yacht)
Cast on 10sts in yarn C (B).
Next row: Inc 1st, k to last 2sts, inc 1st, k1. (12sts)
Next row: K.
Rep last 2 rows × 2. (16sts)
Leave yarn C (B) at side and join yarn B (C).
K 2 rows.
Break yarn B (C).
K 2 rows in yarn C (B).

Sail (Make 10)
Cast on 16sts in yarn A.
1st row: K.
Next row: P2tog, p to last 2sts, p2tog. (14sts)
Next row: K1, k2tog, k to last 3sts, skpo, k1. (12sts)
Work 3 rows in st st beg with a p row.
Rep last 4 rows × 2. (8sts)
Next row: K1, k2tog, k to last 3sts, skpo, k1. (6sts)

Next row: P2tog, p2, p2tog. (4sts)
Next row: K2tog, skpo. (2sts)
Next row: P2tog. (1st)
Break yarn and pull through rem st.

Making up
Place two hull pieces together with the right sides facing inwards and oversew around the sides and base. Turn the piece the right way out.

Stuff lightly and sew the top seam using mattress stitch (see p.240).

Cut five triangles from the white craft foam using the template, below. Place two sail pieces together with the right sides facing inwards and oversew the two sides. Turn the sail the right way out. Insert a triangle of craft foam into the sail and oversew across the lower edge. Using pale grey embroidery thread or thin pale grey yarn, work a line of running stitch down the centre of the front and back of the sails, using the photograph as a guide.

Cut 5 diamonds from red felt using the template, below.

Smooth the two lengths of wire. Use the pliers to make a small loop at each end of the two wires – but

leave a slight gap in each loop. Cut 4 x 60cm (23½in) lengths of beading thread. Using the thread double, take it down the yacht from the top of the sail to the bottom of the hull of the two yachts in yarn B and two of the yachts in yarn C, so that there is a 15cm (6in) long loop of thread at the top of the yachts. Secure the thread at the bottom of the hulls and trim.

Loop the yachts onto the loops at the end of the wires and close the loops. The two yachts in yarn B should be at the ends of one wire and the two yachts in yarn C at the ends of the other wire.

Using the remaining 1.1m (43in) of beading thread double, take it up through the remaining yacht in yarn C from the bottom of the hull to

the top of the sail. Tie the doubled thread in a knot at the top of the sail and again 16cm (6¼in) further on. Use the remaining thread to secure the two wires together at their centres and to create a loop for hanging the mobile.

Apply a thin layer of glue to each of the red felt diamonds. Fold them in half around the beading thread at the top of the sail to form the flags.

Diamond (flag)   **Triangle (sail)**

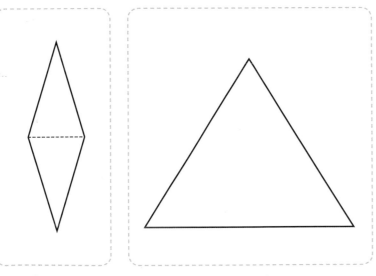

Trace the templates above on to tracing paper and cut them out instead of using the template straight from the book. That way, you can avoid any mistakes and keep the original template intact.

The felt flags are glued in place around the beading thread. Make sure the edges are lined up and the flag is straight before the glue dries.

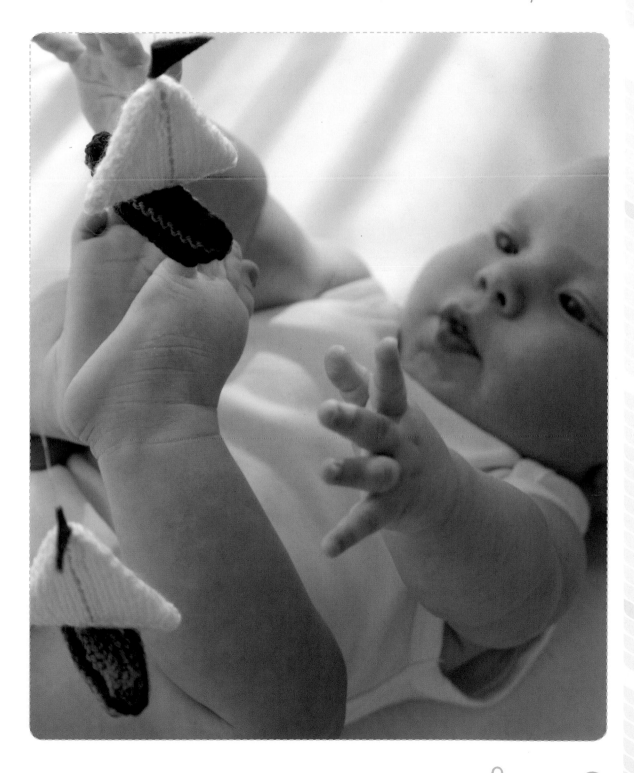

you will need

size
62 × 87cm (24½ × 34¼in)

materials
Rowan Cashsoft DK
50g in
Lime (509) × 7
1 pair of 4mm (UK8/US6)
needles
Large-eyed needle

tension
22sts and 30 rows to 10cm
(4in) over patt on 4mm
(UK8/US6) needles

Diamond blanket

THIS IS AN IDEAL PROJECT for improving your knitting and purling skills. You don't have to follow any complex charts to create the attractive diamond pattern, you just need to be able to create basic knit and purl stitches. A double-sided moss stitch is used to border the blanket and prevent the edges from curling.

how to make

Bottom border
Cast on 137sts.
Moss st row: [K1, p1] to last st, k1.
This row forms moss st.
Rep the row × 5.

Commence pattern
Row 1 (RS): [K1, p1] × 2, k4, *p1, k7, rep from * to last 9sts, p1, k4, [p1, k1] × 2.
Rows 2 and 8: [K1, p1] × 2, p3, *k1, p1, k1, p5, rep from * to last 10sts,

k1, p1, k1, p3, [p1, k1] × 2.
Rows 3 and 7: [K1, p1] × 2, k2, *p1, k3, rep from * to last 7sts, p1, k2, [p1, k1] × 2.
Rows 4 and 6: [K1, p1] × 2, p1, *k1, p5, k1, p1, rep from * to last 4sts, [p1, k1] × 2.
Row 5: [K1, p1] × 2, *p1, k7, rep from * to last 5sts, p1, [p1, k1] × 2.
Rep rows 1–8 until work measures 84cm (33in) from cast on edge, ending with row 8.

Top border
Moss stitch row: [K1, p1] to last st, k1.
This row forms moss st.
Rep this row × 5.
Cast off in patt.
Darn in ends on WS and block according to ballband instructions.

This subtle knit and purl texture adds interest. Very dark colours may disguise a great deal of carefully created detail, so try to choose a yarn colour that will show off your hard work.

The benefit of using a knit and purl stitch pattern is that the reverse side of the work will feature a negative relief image of the right side. This makes it double-sided – perfect for blankets.

A moss stitch edging is used to help the blanket to lie flat and also adds a soft frame to the finished piece. This edging is easy to create and looks very attractive.

you will need

size
Width 41cm (16in)
Length 71cm (28in)

materials
Wendy Supreme Luxury
Cotton Chunky 100g in
A: Pale Blue (1422) x 5
Wendy Supreme Luxury
Cotton DK 100g in
B: Seashell (1946) x 1
C: Cream (1851) x 1
D: Lime (1928) x 1
1 pair of 6mm (UK4/US10)
needles
1 pair of 3.25mm (UK10/
US3) needles
Safety pin
Small oddment of black
yarn for embroidering eyes
on fish

tension
14sts and 20 rows to 10cm
(4in) over st st on 6mm
(UK4/US10) needles
Tension is not critical on
this project

Toy tidy

BOTH TIME AND PATIENCE WILL BE WELL REWARDED when you have completed this lovely toy tidy for the nursery. The main piece and pockets are knitted in chunky yarn whilst the appliquéd fish, starfish, and seaweed are knitted in a finer weight yarn. Be sure to hang it high enough so that your baby won't be able to pull it down.

❧ how to make

Main piece
Using 6mm (UK4/US10) needles, cast on 51sts in yarn A.
Work 4 rows in g st.
Begin pattern:
Rows 1–4 (RS): Beg with a k row, work in st st.
Row 5: *P3, k3 rep from * to the last 3sts, p3.
Row 6: P.
Rep last 2 rows x 1, then row 5 x 1.
Work 4 rows in st st, beg with a p row.
Row 14: P3, *k3, p3 rep from * to end.
Row 15: K.
Rep last 2 rows x 1, then row 14 x 1.
These 18 rows form the pattern and are repeated.
Cont in patt until work measures 69cm (27in) from beg, ending on a WS row.
Work 8 rows g st and cast off. This is the top of the tidy.
Starting at top edge using 6mm (UK4/US10) needles and yarn A, pick up and k 1st from every row end along one side edge (see p.238). K 3 rows g st and cast off fairly firmly.
Rep on other long side edge.

Large pockets (Make 2)
Using 6mm (UK4/US10) needles, cast on 40sts in yarn A.
Work 3 rows g st.
Next row: K.
Next row: K3, p to last 3sts, k3.
Cont as on last 2 rows for a further 24 rows.
Work 5 rows g st.
Cast off.

Small pocket
Using 6mm (UK4/US10) needles, cast on 36sts in yarn A.
Work 3 rows g st.
Next row: K.
Next row: K3, p to last 3sts, k3.
Cont as on last 2 rows for a further 24 rows.
Work 5 rows g st.
Cast off.

Hanging loops (Make 3)
Using 6mm (UK4/US10) needles, cast on 4sts in yarn A.
K 1 row.
Inc 1st at each end of next and following alt rows to 12sts.
K 22 rows.
Cast off.

Fish (Make 2 large and 2 small)
Size for larger fish given in brackets.
Using 3.25mm (UK10/US3) needles, cast on 2sts in yarn C.
Row 1 and all alt rows: K.
Row 2: K1, inc in next st. (3sts)
Row 4: Inc in first st, k1, inc in last st. (5sts)
Row 6: Inc in first st, k3, inc in last st. (7sts)
Cont to inc as before until you have 15 (19) sts on the needle.
Next row: K.
Change to yarn B and k 4 rows.
Change to yarn C and k 6 rows.
Change to yarn B and k 4 rows.
Change to yarn C and k 2 rows.
Now dec 1st at each end of next and foll alt rows until 7 (9) sts remain.
K 1 row.
Next row: Inc in each st to end. (14 (18) sts)

Next row: K.
Next row: Inc at each end of row.
(16 (20) sts)
K 3 rows.
Cast off.

Single seaweed piece (Make 3)
Using 3.25mm (UK10/US3) needles,
cast on 5sts in yarn D.
Work 6 rows g st.
** Next row: K.
Next row: K2, p1, k2.
Rep last row for desired length.
Next row: K2tog, k1, k2tog.
Next row: K3tog. Fasten off **.

Double seaweed piece
Using 3.25mm (UK10/US3) needles,
cast on 10sts in yarn D.
Work 6 rows g st.
Next row: Work 5sts, turn and leave
remaining 5 sts on spare safety pin.
Cont on these sts and work from **
to ** as on Single seaweed piece.
Return to sts on safety pin and work
to match first piece.

Starfish (Make 5)
The starfish is knitted as five pieces
and then joined together.
Using 3.25mm (UK10/US3) needles,
cast on 2sts in yarn B.
Next row: K.
Next row: K1, inc in next st. (3sts)
Next row: P1, k1, p1.
Next row: Inc in next st, p1, inc in
next st.
Next row: P2, k1, p2.
Next row: Inc in next st, k1, p1, k1,
inc in next st.
Next row: P3, k1, p3.
Next row: Inc in next st, k2, p1, k2,
inc in next st.

Next row: P4, k1, p4.
Next row: K4, p1, k4.
Rep the last 2 rows × 1. Leave sts on
a spare needle.

To join sections together:
Next row: Work across first section
as follows: P4, k1, p4, work across
rem four sections in the same way.
(45sts)
Next row: K4, p1, *k8, p1 rep from *
to last 4sts, k4.
Next row: P2, p2tog, k1. *P2tog × 4,
k1, rep from * 3 times more, p2tog,
p2. (27sts)
Next row: K3, p1, *k4, p1 rep from *
3 times more, k3.
Next row: K1, p2tog, *k1, p2tog × 2,
rep from * to last 4sts, k1, p2tog, k1.
Break yarn and run thread through
sts on needles, draw up to form star,
secure and fasten off.

Bubbles
Using 3.25mm (UK10/US3) needles,
cast on 12sts in yarn C, cast off
loosely. When stitching in place wind
the piece of knitting into a circle and
secure with a few stitches.

Making up
Take main piece and work in any
loose ends of yarn neatly (see p.242).
Lay piece on a flat surface. Take the
hanging loops and pin them evenly
in position along the top edge. Sew
them in place on each side of the
work to form the loops.

Take the pockets and pin them in
position onto the main piece. The
smaller pocket will be at the top
and the other two are evenly spaced

top tip
Take your time
and sew neatly
when attaching
small pieces.

below. Sew each pocket in place along
three sides. Catch the centre of each
large pocket to the main piece to
stop the pockets sagging open.

Take fish and work in all ends. Take a
piece of yarn C and a sewing needle,
working from the centre of the tail
run a thread through to the base of
the tail, draw up slightly to indent
the tail and fasten off.

Using black yarn embroider eyes on
fish by making a French knot.

Arrange the fish, starfish, and
seaweed in a pleasing pattern onto
the main piece. Follow the photo as
a guide, or use your imagination and
arrange your own display. When you
are happy with the layout, stitch each
piece carefully in place. Twist the
seaweed (see main image) to give it
a more realistic look when sewing it
in place. Make sure you don't sew
through both thicknesses of the
pockets as you work.

Arrange bubbles by some of the
fish's mouths then sew them in place.

There are two different sizes of fish in this pattern. Make two of each size. The bubbles are knitted as a long strip that is coiled and stitched in place.

The starfish is knitted in five sections which are then joined together. If you want to add more than one starfish, simply knit another.

The hanging loops are knitted as separate strips and stitched in place along the top edge to form the loop. Make sure they are securely attached.

Secure the centre of each large pocket to the main, back piece to prevent the pocket from sagging open. If you wish to create divisions in the pockets, stitch all the way down the length of the pocket with a running stitch before you attach any of the details. Try not to overload your toy tidy or it will stretch the knitting out of shape and sag.

For *Classic socks* see pages 166–169

Elephant cushion

THIS ELEPHANT-MOTIF CUSHION IS CREATED using the intarsia technique (see pp.233–235). The elephant's ear is knitted separately and sewn on afterwards, along with a three-dimensional tassel tail. If you'd like to give your elephant an eye, as we've done, all you need is a small amount of felt and embroidery thread in the colour of your choice.

🌿 you will need

size
40cm (16in) square

materials
Debbie Bliss Cotton DK
50g in
A: Green (060) × 4
B: Cream (002) × 1
C: Pink (049) × 2
1 pair of 4mm (UK8/US6)
needles
Yarn bobbins
Large-eyed needle
40cm (16in) square
cushion pad
Crochet hook (optional)
Small circle of felt (optional)
Embroidery thread (optional)
Sewing needle (optional)

tension
20sts and 30 rows to 10cm
(4in) over patt on 4mm (UK8/US6) needles

🌿 how to make

Front
Cast on 80sts in yarn A.
Row 1 (RS): K to end.
Row 2: P to end.
Rep rows 1 and 2 until 28 rows worked.
Row 29: Follow the Elephant chart (see p.128) until patt knitted.
Row 77: K to end.
Row 78: P to end.
Rep rows 77 and 78 and cont until 28 rows are knitted.
Cast off.

Back (Make 2)
Cast on 80sts in yarn A and cont as follows:
Row 1 (RS): *K to end.
Row 2: P to end.
Row 3: Rep from * until 46 rows are knitted.
Row 47: *Change to yarn C and k to end.
Row 48: K.
Row 49: Change to yarn B and k to end.
Row 50: K.
Rep from * until 20 rows knitted in total.

Ear piece
Cast on 27sts in yarn C.
Row 1 (RS): K to end.
Row 2: K to end.
Row 3: K to st 27 then inc 1st. (28sts)
Rows 4–6: K to end.
Row 7: K to st 28 then inc 1st. (29sts)
Rows 8–11: K to end.
Row 12: K to st 27 then k2tog. (28sts)
Row 13: K to end.
Row 14: K2tog, k to st 24 then k2tog. (26sts)
Row 15: K to end.
Row 16: K2tog, k2tog, k to st 22, k2tog. (23sts)
Row 17: K2tog, k to end. (22sts)
Row 18: K2tog, k to st 22, k2tog. (20sts)
Row 19: K2tog, k to end. (19sts)
Row 20: K2tog, k to st 19, k2tog. (17sts)
Row 21: K2tog, k to end. (16sts)
Row 22: K2tog, k2tog, k to st 12, k2tog. (13sts)
Row 23: K2tog, k to st 10 then k2tog. (11sts)
Row 24: K2tog, k to st 5, k2tog, k2tog. (8sts)
Row 25: K to end.
Cast off.

Making up

Lay all pieces flat, RS together, and check that each side measures 40cm (16in). For the two back panel pieces, overlap the striped edges and backstitch around the edges (see p.242).

Attach the ear

Place the cast on edge on the diagonal from the edge of the tusk to the top of the head. Use mattress stitch (see p.240) to attach the ear along the underneath of the cast on edge so the stitches are invisible.

Tassel tail

Cut 20cm (8in) lengths of yarns A, B, and C, fold them in half and using a crochet hook or the tip of your needle, pull the folded section through from the back to the front where you want the tail to be positioned. Do the same with the bottom of the tail a few rows below. Pull the bottom of the tail through the loop. (See p.246 for more information on attaching a fringe.)

Eye (optional)

You can give your elephant an eye, as we have, by cutting a small circle of felt to the size you want your eye to be. With a sewing needle and embroidery thread, create a French knot in the centre of the circle of felt. Sew the eye securely in place.

Insert the cushion pad.

Elephant chart

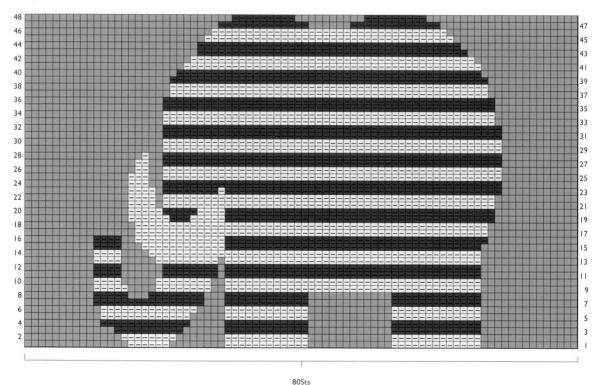

80Sts

☐ Stocking st (k 1 row, p 1 row)
⊟ Garter st (k every row)
▨ Green
☐ Cream
■ Pink

top tip

Use small pieces of card if you don't have any yarn bobbins.

Attach the elephant's tail as you would attach a fringe (see p.246). You can make the tail multi-coloured, as above, or just use one colour.

The ear is sewn on from underneath using mattress stitch (see p.240). Attaching it in this way means that the stitches are not seen.

Insert the cushion pad inside the knitted cover, then overlap the striped edges to close. Alternatively, you can sew on a few press studs to keep your cushion cover closed (see p.243). Make sure there are no sharp edges on the press studs.

Ice cream sundae
blanket

DELICIOUS SHADES AND A SOFT TOUCH YARN are used to create this delightful chunky blanket to keep baby cosy and snug on even the coolest days. Knitted on big needles and using a small, four-row-repeat pattern, this blanket is ideal for a novice who wants to experiment with new stitch combinations involving increases and decreases.

🌿 you will need

size
60cm (23½in) wide × 80cm (31½in) long

materials
King Cole Comfort Chunky 100g in
A: Grape (420) × 2
B: Cream (426) × 2
C: Lemon (422) × 2
D: Ice (424) × 2
1 pair of 5.5mm (UK5/US9) needles

tension
Tension is not critical on this project

🌿 how to make

Using yarn A cast on 92sts.
Work 3 rows in g st.

Commence pattern
Row 1 (RS): K1, [k2tog] × 3, [yfwd, k1] × 6, * [skpo] × 3, [k2tog] × 3, [yfwd, k1] × 6, rep from * to last 7sts, [skpo] × 3, k1.
Rows 2–4: K.
The last 4 rows form the patt and are repeated throughout.

Continue in yarn A until work measures approximately 20cm (8in) ending on Row 2 of pattern.

Change to yarn B and continue for a further 20cm (8in) again ending on Row 2 of pattern.

Continue in this manner with yarn C and yarn D.

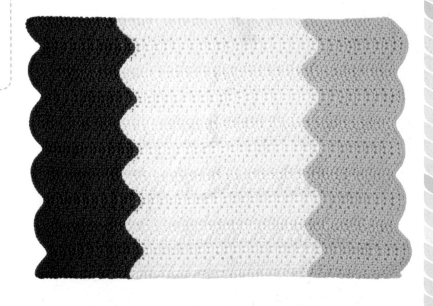

We have used wide stripes in four colours of yarn, but if you wish you can use only one or two colours for your blanket. Remember to change your yarn quantities as required.

top tip

For more information on increases and decreases see pages 219–227.

After completing the fourth stripe work a further 3 rows in g st in yarn D and cast off.

Using a large-eyed needle, work in ends of yarn neatly along the sides of the blanket by weaving them in and out of the knitted fabric (see p.242, Darning in an end).

For this blanket we've worked with a synthetic yarn, but if you'd prefer to use an all-natural yarn you can substitute any chunky weight yarn with few repercussions, as the specific yarn tension is not critical when making this project.

Clever increases and decreases create a neat, scalloped pattern. You can change yarn colours more frequently if you want more stripes in your blanket.

Owl mobile

HANG THESE LITTLE OWLS over your baby's changing table to keep her entertained. Their bright-coloured bodies and large eyes are sure to keep her attention. Remember, never hang your mobile where your baby can reach it. Mobiles are not toys and you should always supervise babies and children when they are around mobiles to avoid any accidents.

🌿 you will need

size
Each owl is approximately 7cm (2¾in) tall

materials
Sublime Baby Cashmere Merino Silk DK 50g in
A: Pebble (006) × 1
B: Carrots (219) × 1
C: Puffin (246) × 1
D: Pinkaboo (162) × 1
1 pair of 3.25mm (UK10/ US3) needles
Toy filling
10 × 1.5mm (¹⁄₁₆in) cream felt circles
Dark grey embroidery thread
2 × 32cm (12½in) lengths of 14-gauge silver wire
3.5m (137in) of 3mm (⅛in) beading thread
Blunt-ended needle
Round-nose jewellery pliers

tension
Tension is not critical on this project

🌿 how to make

Make two owls with bodies in yarn B, two owls with bodies in yarn C, and one owl with a body in yarn D. The heads for all the owls are knitted in yarn A.

Body and head (Make 2)
Cast on 14sts in the yarn B (C:D).
Work 4 rows in st st beg with a k row.
K 2 rows.
Work 2 rows in st st beg with a k row.
K 2 rows.
Rep last 4 rows × 2.
Break yarn B (C:D) and join yarn A.
Work 2 rows in st st beg with a k row.
Next row: K2, M1, k10, M1, k2. (16sts)
Work 6 rows in st st beg with a p row.
Next row: K.
Cast off.

Wings (Make 2)
Cast on 8sts in yarn B (C:D).
K 4 rows.
Next row: K2tog, k4, ssk. (6sts)
Next row: K.
Next row: K2tog, k2, ssk. (4sts)
Next row: K.
Next row: [K2tog] × 2.
Next row: K2tog.
Break yarn and pull through rem st.

Making up

Join the side seams and lower seam using mattress stitch (see p.240). Stuff the owl lightly and oversew the seam at the top of the head. Oversew the wings in place at the top of the body. The wings should wrap around the sides of the owl.

Using three strands of dark grey embroidery thread, secure the eyes in place with six straight stitches. Each stitch should come from the centre of the eye to just over the outer edge. Work a French knot in the centre of each eye.

Using the full six strands of dark grey embroidery thread, work two straight stitches for the beak. Then work another two straight stitches over the ones just worked.

Smooth the two lengths of wire. Use the jewellery pliers to make a small loop at each end of the two wires, leaving a slight gap in each loop.

Cut 4 x 60cm (23½in) lengths of beading thread. Using the thread double, take it down the owl from the top to the bottom of the two

owls in yarn B and two owls in yarn C, so that there is a 14cm (5½in) long loop of thread at the top of the owls. Secure the thread at the bottom of each owl and trim.

Loop the owls onto the loops at the end of the wires and close the wire loops. The two owls in yarn B should be at the ends of one wire and the two owls in yarn C at the ends of the other wire.

Using the remaining 1.1m (43in) of beading thread double, take it up through the owl in yarn D from the bottom to the top. Tie the doubled thread in a knot at the top of the owl and again 15cm (6in) further on. Use the remaining thread to secure the two wires together at their centres and to create a loop for hanging the mobile.

Be sure to hang the mobile well out of reach of babies and children and do not leave your child unattended around the mobile. Do not hang the mobile above your baby's cot. Ensure that the mobile is securely attached and will not fall on or be pulled down by your baby.

top tip

You can knit and make up one owl on its own to be used as a small toy.

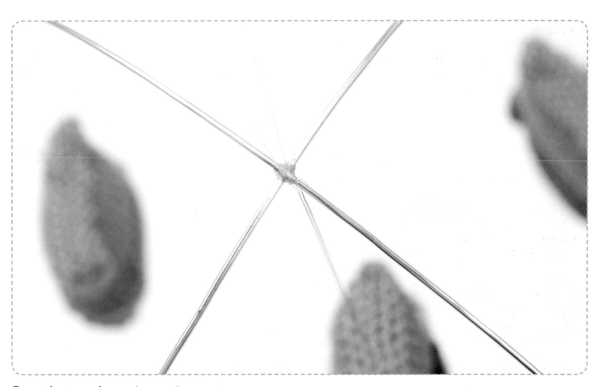

Cross the two wires and secure them together, evenly, in the centre with the beading thread.

Each owl's body is knitted using a four row stocking stitch, two row knit pattern to give it texture that looks like feathers. The owl's head is knitted in stocking stitch.

The owl's eyes are created using a felt disk that is sewn in place with six long, straight stitches and a central French knot.

Colourful bunting

A BRIGHT, FESTIVE ADDITION TO ANY ROOM, this colourful bunting is knitted using garter stitch. Knit the flags in colours to match your child's room. Choose as many or as few colours as you'd like, just be sure to adjust your yarn requirements if needed. Securely hang the bunting somewhere it cannot be pulled down by babies or children and cause a hazard.

🌿 you will need

size
Length approximately
2.4m (94in)

materials
Rowan Belle Organic DK by
Amy Butler 50g in
A: Moonflower (013) × 1
B: Dahlia (029)× 1
C: Robin's egg (014) × 1
D: Clementine (020) × 1
E: Concord (035) × 1
F: Dew (025) × 1
1 pair of 4mm (UK8/US6)
needles
Large-eyed needle

tension
22sts and 30 rows to 10cm
(4in) over g st on 4mm
(UK8/US6) needles

🌿 how to make

Ribbon string
Cast on 512sts in yarn A.
Now cast them off by knitting
2sts together into the back of the
stitches. Tie off yarn end and weave
yarn ends in neatly (see p.242,
Darning in an end).

Pendant flags
For the first flag, count 20sts from
the end of ribbon and then pick up
22sts (see p.238–239).
Join in yarn B.
K 1 row
Next begin pattern as follows:
Row 1: S1, k2tog, k to last 3sts,
k2tog, k1.
Rows 2–4: S1, k to end of row.
Rep rows 1–4 until 6sts remain
after 4th row.
Next row: S1, [k2tog] × 2, k1. (4sts)
Next row: S1, k to end of row.
Next row: S1, k to end of row.
Next row: S1, k to end of row.
Next row: S1, k2tog, k1. (3sts)
Next row: S1, k2tog. (2sts)
Next row: K2tog. (1st)
Cast off.

Making up
Break yarn leaving enough spare to tie
off tight and thread yarn through large-
eyed needle. Weave end in neatly up
the edge of the RS of the pendant.
Weave in the initial cast on yarn end.

Now leave 3sts gap on your ribbon
and pick up the next 22sts. Repeat
previous instructions for this and all
subsequent flags. The repeating
colour sequence we've used here
is: yarns B, C, D, E, and F.

Pick up stitches from the same side
of the ribbon for each flag so the WS
is consistent across the entire length.

size
72.5cm x 1m (28½ x 39in)

materials
Sublime Extra Fine Merino Wool
DK 50g in
Bone (251) x 11
1 pair of 4mm (UK8/US6)
needles
Large-eyed needle

tension
22sts and 28 rows to 10cm (4in)
over little check stitch patt on
4mm (UK8/US6) needles

special pattern
Little check stitch:
Row 1: *K5, p5, rep from * to last
5sts, k5.
Row 2: P.
Repeat last 2 rows x 2, then
row 1.
Row 8: K5, *p5, k5, rep from *
to end.
Row 9: K.
Rep last 2 rows x 2, then row 8.

Checked
squares blanket

A HAND-KNITTED COT BLANKET is one of the most cherished items in a child's early years. This blanket is worked using areas of little check stitch on a ground of garter stitch. The little checked stitch pattern is worked across a multiple of 10 stitches, plus five extra stitches. The ruffled border is worked in stocking stitch to complete the project.

how to make

Cast on 169sts.
Row 1 (RS): P.
Row 2: P.
Row 3: P2, s1 p1 psso, p to last 4sts, p2tog, p2. (167sts)
Row 4: P.
Row 5 and every alt row: K2, s1 k2tog psso, k to last 5sts, k3tog tbl, k2.
Row 6 and every alt row: P.
Rep rows 5 and 6 until 127sts remain.
Row 25: S1 [25sts from little check stitch patt, k25] × 2, 25sts from little check stitch patt, k1.
Row 26: S1, [p25, k25] × 2, p26.
Rows 27–30: [Rep rows 25 and 26] × 2.
Row 31: As row 25.
Row 32: S1, [25sts from little check stitch patt, k25] × 1, 25sts from little check stitch patt, k1.
Row 33: S1, k to end.
Rows 34–37: [Rep rows 32 and 33] × 2.
Row 38: As row 33.
Rows 39–52: Rep rows 25–38.
Row 53: S1, [k25, 25sts from little check stitch patt] × 2, k26.
Cont to work with the patt blocks set in this way until you have made 11 reps of the squares.
Row 333 and every foll alt row: S1, k1, inc 2sts in next st, inc 1st in next st, k to last 4sts, inc 1st in next st, inc 2sts in next st, k2.

Row 334 and every foll alt row: S1, p2 pass second st on LH needle over first st, p to last 5sts, put point of RH needle through first st on LH needle and p second st, passing both loops off needle together, p3.
Row 352: S1, p1, inc in next st, pass second st on LH needle over first st, p to last 5sts, put point of RH needle through first st on LH needle and p second st, passing both loops off needle together, inc in next st, p2.
Rows 353–355: P.
Cast off.

Side panels
With RS facing, pick up and k294 evenly along straight side edge.
Row 1 (WS): P.
Row 2: As row 333.
Row 3: As row 334.
Rows 4–21: Rep rows 2 and 3.
Rows 22–24: P.
Cast off.
Rep on opposite straight edge.

Making up
Neatly sew up the corner shaping and then sew in all of the yarn tails. Press gently, encouraging the border to ruffle (see p.240, Blocking).

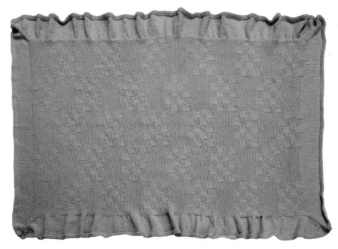

Accessories

Cross-over booties

USE SIMPLE SHAPES AND AN EASY 1-ROW PATTERN in moss stitch to create these pretty little shoes that will keep baby's feet warm. Complete the look with clusters of cute roses and rosebuds embroidered in bright contrasting shades using bullion stitch and lazy daisy stitch. Cast off your knitting loosely for a delicate, soft top edge to the shoes.

how to make

Moss stitch row 1: *K1, p1, rep from * to last st, k1.

Repeat last row to create the stitch pattern. If you are not familiar with this stitch try a little test piece to get used to working the stitch.

Please note: When increasing stitches, take care to maintain the continuity of the pattern as you do.

Shoe (Make 2)
Begin with sole of shoes as follows:
Cast on 7sts, work 2 rows in moss stitch (as above).
Keeping continuity of the moss stitch pattern throughout, begin to shape sole as follows:
Next row: Inc 1st at each end of the row. (9sts)
Next row: Work in moss st.
Next row: Inc 1st at each end of the row. (11sts)
Work 5 rows straight in moss st.
Next row: Inc 1st at each end of the row. (13sts)
Work 10 rows straight.
Next row: Inc 1st at each end of the row. (15sts)

Work 14 rows straight.
Now begin to shape toe as follows:
Next row: Work 2tog at each end of the row. (13sts)
Next row: Work in moss stitch.
Now work 2tog at each end of the next 3 rows. (7sts)
Cast off.

Upper part of shoe
Cast on 55sts loosely.
Work 13 rows moss st.

Shape over-laps
Next row: Work 2tog at each end of the row. (53sts)
Next row: Rep previous row. (51sts)
Next row: Work in moss st.
Next row: Work 2tog at each end of the row. (49sts)
Rep last 2 rows once more. (47sts)
Cast off.

Making up
Take the upper part of the shoe and pin in place around the outer edge of the sole. Overlap the two ends at the front of the shoe, left over right on one shoe and right over left on the other. Sew in place carefully easing

a little if needed at the rounded toe end of the shoe. Using contrast yarns embroider tiny bullion stitch roses and lazy daisy stitch leaves (see p.244) on either side of the toes.

Wrap the yarn four times round the needle for a rosebud and six for each knot within the main flower. Pull the needle gently through the yarn for a neat finish.

Long, striped hat

PERFECT FOR GIRLS AND BOYS, this long, pointed hat is adorable, and warm for the colder months. We've used a 100 per cent wool yarn, but you can choose any DK weight yarn you'd like to work with if you can achieve the correct tension. Choose colours that complement one another for a softer look, or colours that clash for a wilder look.

top tip
When choosing a yarn look at the fibre content, not just the colour.

you will need

size
Age 0–6 (6–12:12–18: 18–24: 24–36) months
Actual measurements:
Circumference
39:42:44:47:49cm
(15½:16½:17½:18½:19½in)
Length
34:38:40:43:47cm
(13½:15:16:17:18½in)

materials
King Cole Merino Blend DK 50g in
A: Linden (165) × 1 (1:1:2:2)
B: Turquoise (018) × 1 (1:1:1:2)
1 pair of 3.25mm (UK10/US3) needles
1 pair of 4mm (UK8/US6) needles

tension
22sts and 28 rows to 10cm (4in) over st st on 4mm (UK8/US6) needles

special instruction
cable cast on: Work as a Knit-on cast on (see p.208), but after the second stitch is made, insert needle between last two stitches to make each new one

how to make

Ribbed edge
Using 3.25mm (UK10/US3) needles and yarn A, cast on 86 (92:96:102: 108) sts using cable cast on method, see below.
Row 1: P2 (0:0:2:0), *k2, p2, rep from * to end.
Row 2: *K2, p2, rep from * to last 2 (0:0:2:0) sts, k2 (0:0:2:0).
These 2 rows form 2 × 2 rib.
Work 4 (6:6:8:8) further rows in 2 × 2 rib.
Change to 4mm (UK8/US6) needles and yarn B and beg with a k row, work 2 rows in st st.
Change to yarn A and beg with a k row, work 2 rows in st st.
These 4 rows form stripe sequence.
Cont in stripe sequence throughout (carrying each yarn up the side of the work when changing colour, see p.233, tidying edges) and beg with a k row, work in st st until hat measures 10 (11:12:13:14)cm (4 (4¼:5:5¼: 5½)in) from beg, ending with a p row.

Shape the point
Keeping stripe sequence correct as set, cont as follows:
Row 1 (RS): K2tog, [k26 (28:29:31:33) k2tog] × 2, k26 (28:30:32:34), k2tog. (82 (88:92:98:104) sts)
Beg with a p row, work 3 rows in st st.
Row 5: K2tog, [k24 (26:28:30:32) k2tog] × 2, k26 (28:28:30:32), k2tog. (78 (84:88:94:100) sts)
Beg with a p row, work 3 rows in st st.
Row 9: K2tog, [k23 (25:26:28:30) k2tog] × 2, k24 (26:28:30:32), k2tog. (74 (80:84:90:96) sts)
Beg with a p row, work 3 rows in st st.
Row 13: K2tog, [k22 (24:25:27:29) k2tog] × 2, k22 (24:26:28:30), k2tog. (70 (76:80:86:92) sts)
Beg with a p row, work 3 rows in st st.

Row 17: K2tog, [k20 (22:24:26:28), k2tog] × 2, k22 (24:24:26:28), k2tog. (66 (72:76:82:88) sts)
Beg with a p row, work 3 rows in st st.
Row 21: K2tog, [k19 (21:22:24:26) k2tog] × 2, k20 (22:24:26:28), k2tog. (62 (68:72:78:84) sts)
Beg with a p row, work 3 rows in st st.
Row 25: K2tog, [k18 (20:21:23:25) k2tog] × 2, k18 (20:22:24:26), k2tog. (58 (64:68:74:80) sts)
Beg with a p row, work 3 rows in st st.
Row 29: K2tog, [k16 (18:20:22:24) k2tog] × 2, k18 (20:20:22:24), k2tog. (54 (60:64:70:76) sts)
Beg with a p row, work 3 rows in st st.
Row 33: K2tog, [k15 (17:18:20:22) k2tog] × 2, k16 (18:20:22:24), k2tog. (50 (56:60:66:72) sts)
Beg with a p row, work 3 rows in st st.
Row 37: K2tog, [k14 (16:17:19:21) k2tog] × 2, k14 (16:18:20:22), k2tog. (46 (52:56:62:68) sts)
Beg with a p row, work 3 rows in st st.
Row 41: K2tog, [k12 (14:16:18:20) k2tog] × 2, k14 (16:16:18:20), k2tog. (42 (48:52:58:64) sts)
Beg with a p row, work 3 rows in st st.
Row 45: K2tog, [k11 (13:14:16:18) k2tog] × 2, k12 (14:16:18:20), k2tog. (38 (44:48:54:60) sts)
Beg with a p row, work 3 rows in st st.
Row 49: K2tog, [k10 (12:13:15:17) k2tog] × 2, k10 (12:14:16:18), k2tog. (34 (40:44:50:56) sts)
Beg with a p row, work 3 rows in st st.
Row 53: K2tog, [k8 (10:12:14:16) k2tog] × 2, k10 (12:12:14:16), k2tog. (30 (36:40:46:52) sts)

For 2nd, 3rd, 4th, and 5th sizes only:
Beg with a p row, work 3 rows in st st.
Row 57: K2tog, [k (9:10:12:14) k2tog] × 2, k (10:12:14:16), k2tog. ((32:36:42:48) sts)

Beg with a p row, work 3 rows in st st.
Row 61: K2tog, [k (8:9:11:13), k2tog]
× 2, k (8:10:12:14), k2tog.
((28:32:38:44) sts)
Beg with a p row, work 3 rows in st st.
Row 65: K2tog, [k (6:8:10:12), k2tog]
× 2, k (8:8:10:12), k2tog.
((24:28:34:40) sts)

For 4th and 5th sizes only:
Beg with a p row, work 3 rows in st st.
Row 69: K2tog, [k (8:10), k2tog] × 2,
k (10:12), k2tog. ((30:36) sts)
Beg with a p row, work 3 rows in st st.
Row 73: K2tog, [k (7:9), k2tog] × 2,
k (8:10), k2tog. ((26:32) sts)

For 5th size only:
Beg with a p row, work 3 rows in st st.
Row 77: K2tog, [k8, k2tog] × 3. (28sts)
Beg with a p row, work 3 rows in st st.
Row 81: K2tog, [k6, k2tog] × 2, k8,
k2tog. (24sts)

For 1st and 3rd sizes only:
P 1 row.
Next row: K2tog, [k7 (6), k2tog] × 2,
k8 (8), k2tog. (26 (24) sts)

All sizes:
P 1 row.
Next row: K2tog, [k6 (5:5:6:5),
k2tog] × 2, k6 (6:6:6:6), k2tog.
(22 (20:20:22:20) sts)
P 1 row.
Next row: K2tog, [k4 (4:4:4:4),
k2tog] × 2, k6 (4:4:6:4), k2tog.
(18 (16:16:18:16) sts)
P 1 row.
Next row: K2tog, [k3 (2:2:3:2),
k2tog] × 2, k4 (4:4:4:4), k2tog.
(14 (12:12:14:12) sts)
P 1 row.
Next row: K2tog, [k2 (1:1:2:1),
k2tog] × 2, k2 (2:2:2:2), k2tog.
(10 (8:8:10:8) sts)
Next row: [P2tog] × 5 (4:4:5:4).

(5 (4:4:5:4) sts)
Break off yarn leaving a long tail and
draw this through rem sts twice, pull
up tightly. Use this end to sew the
centre back seam using mattress stitch
(see p.240).

Making up
Sew in all ends. Make a tassel by
wrapping yarn B around the first
three fingers of your hand approx
50 times. Pull a long strand of yarn
between the wrapped yarn and your
fingers and tie it tightly around the
strands. Cut the opposite side. Wrap
another strand of yarn tightly around
the top, a short distance below
where you tied it off. Securely sew
the strand through the wraps and
into the tassel head a few times. Trim
the ends of the tassel so that they
are even. Sew the tassel to the point
of the hat.

Sew the centre back seam using
mattress stitch. Match the stripes as
you work for a clean, almost invisible,
finish to the work.

The tassel should be worked tightly
to keep the strands from loosening
and coming out. Make sure it is sewn
securely to the hat and won't come off.

A 2 x 2 ribbed edge frames the hat
and provides stretch to the edge. Work
this ribbed edge and the tassel in a third
colour yarn to add even more interest.

Newborn mittens

KEEP A NEWBORN BABY WARM and prevent scratches with these thumbless mittens knitted in stocking stitch. Worked in lightweight 4-ply yarn, the mittens are knitted in 100 per cent pure wool so they don't irritate delicate skin. An optional crocheted cord keeps the mittens together so they won't get lost if one falls off.

you will need

size
To fit a newborn baby

materials
Patons Fairytale Dreamtime
4-ply 50g in
A: White (051) × 1
B: Pastel blue (2934) × 1
1 pair of 2.75mm (UK12/US2) needles
1 pair of 3.75mm (UK9/US5) needles
Crochet hook (optional)
Large-eyed needle

tension
28sts and 36 rows to 10cm (4in) over st st on 3.75mm (UK9/US5) needles

how to make

Mittens (Make 2)
Using 2.75mm (UK12/US2) needles and yarn A, cast on 30sts.
Beg k, st st 4 rows.
Next row (RS): Join in yarn B. K1 in yarn B, [k1 in yarn A, k2 in yarn B] to last 2sts, k1 in yarn A, k1 in yarn B.
Cont in patt, carrying yarn not in use across WS of work:
Row 1 (WS): *K1 in yarn B, [p1 in yarn A, k2 in yarn B] to last 2sts, p1 in yarn A, k1 in yarn B.
Row 2: P1 in yarn B, [k1 in yarn A, p2 in yarn B] to last 2sts, k1 in yarn A, p1 in yarn B.*
Rep * to * × 2.
Row 3: As row 1.
Break off yarn B. Change to 3.75mm (UK9/US5) needles and beg k row, cont in st st until work measures 8cm (3in) from beg, ending after p row.

Shape top
Row 1: K1, [k2tog, k3] to last 4sts, k2tog, k2. (24sts)
Row 2: P.
Row 3: K1, [k2tog, k2] to last 3sts, k2tog, k1. (18sts)
Row 4: [P2tog] × 9. (9sts)
Row 5: [K2tog] × 2, k1, [k2tog] × 2. (5sts)

Break yarn, thread end through rem sts, gather up tightly and fasten off.

Making up
Join side seams. If making the cord, use a crochet hook and both yarns together to make a chain and sew one end to the inside of each mitten.

Crocheting a cord
Make a slip knot and slide it onto a crochet hook. With your yarn hand forefinger, yarnover the hook from back to front (see p.223). Slide the yarn from the yarnover into the inner bend of the hook. Pull the hook, carrying the wrapped strand of yarn through the loop on your hook. Repeat to create a chain.

top tip

Thumbless mittens are the easiest type to put on a newborn baby.

Chullo earflap hat

KEEP YOUR CHILD'S EARS WARM during cold days with a hat that includes earflaps. It is knitted in the round using stocking stitch and is totally practical with optional chin ties to stop the hat from being pulled off. This versatile pattern gives four sizes for a hat to fit a child's head circumference from 33cm (13in) up to 48.25cm (19in).

how to make

Earflaps (Make 2)
Cast on 3sts.
Row 1 (RS): K1, kfb, k1. (4sts)
Row 2 (WS): K1, p2, k1.
Row 3: K1, kfb, kfb, k1. (6sts)
Row 4: K1, p4, k1.
Row 5: K1, kfb, k2, kfb, k1. (8sts)
33cm (13in) size jump to row 12.
Row 6: K1, p6, k1.
Row 7: K1, kfb, k4, kfb, k1. (10sts)
38cm (15in) size jump to row 12
Row 8: K1, p8, k1.
Row 9: K1, kfb, k6, kfb, k1. (12sts)
43.25cm (17in) size jump to row 12.
Row 10: K1, p10, k1.
Row 11: K1, kfb, k8, kfb, k1. (14sts)
Row 12: K1, p to last st, k1.
Row 13: K all sts.
Break yarn and hold sts on a stitch holder ready to join to the body. Work second earflap to match. With spare needles and yarn, and knitting across both earflaps with RS facing, and using cable cast on method, work next round as follows: Cast on 5 (5:6:6) sts, k8 (10:12:14) sts from first earflap, cast on 17 (18:19:20) sts, k8 (10:12:14) sts from second earflap, cast on 4 (5:5:6) sts then join in the round taking care not to twist the stitches. (42 (48:54:60) sts)

Body
Work st st until work measures 9 (9.5:10.25:10.75)cm (3½ (3¾:4: 4¼)in)

Shape crown
Round 1: *K4, k2tog; rep from * to end. (35 (40:45:50) sts)
Round 2 and all even rounds: P all sts.
Round 3: *K3, k2tog; rep from * to end. (28 (32:36:40) sts)
Round 5: *K2, k2tog; rep from * to end. (21 (24:27:30) sts)
Round 7: *K1, k2tog; rep from * to end. (14 (16:18:20) sts)
Round 9: *K2tog; rep from * to end. (7 (8:9:10) sts)
Round 11: *K2tog; rep from * to last (1 (0:1:0) sts). (4 (4:5:5) sts)
Break yarn and draw through remaining sts, tighten to close.

Making up
Weave in all ends. Block according to the ballband instructions (see p.240).

Trim (Optional)
Work blanket stitch around the base of the hat. To do this, knot a length of yarn and, using a large-eyed needle, bring it out at the base of the rim from WS to RS. Moving 2sts above

right, take a vertical stitch, looping the yarn under the needle. Repeat around the hat, leaving a 1st gap between each vertical stitch. Insert a crochet hook into the lowest point of the earflap and work a crochet chain for approx. 10cm (4in) to create a tie cord. Break the yarn and tighten to close. Work a second tie to match the other earflap.

Working on double-pointed needles enables you to knit all the way to the crown without leaving a cast off edge, or seams to sew up.

For *Building blocks* see pages 84–85

you will need

size
To fit a child, aged 0–3 months

materials
Sublime Baby Cashmere Merino
Silk DK 50g in
A: Gooseberry (004) × 1
B: Piglet (001) × 1
1 pair of 3.25mm (UK10/US3
needles

Stitch holder
Large-eyed needle
2 × 1cm (½in) pink floral buttons

tension
28sts and 36 rows to 10cm (4in)
over st st on 3.25mm (UK10/
US3) needles

A flower-shaped button
makes a pretty little detail, as
well as secures the strap across
baby's foot so the bootie won't
fall off.

Shoe booties

DELICATE BABY BOOTIES WILL MAKE A GREAT GIFT, or a loving addition to your child's wardrobe. Use this project to practise your increase and decrease skills when shaping the toe and heel of the little shoes. The yarn we've used is made from merino wool, silk, and cashmere for a soft feel, but a cotton yarn would work just as well.

❧ how to make

Right shoe
Cast on 33sts in yarn A.
Row 1: K.
Row 2: K1, M1, k15, M1, k1, M1, k15, M1, k1. (37sts)
Row 3: K.
Row 4: K2, M1, k15, M1, k3, M1, k15, M1, k2. (41sts)
Row 5: K.
Row 6: K3, M1, k15, M1, k5, M1, k15, M1, k3. (45sts)
Row 7: K.
Row 8: K4, M1, k15, M1, k7, M1, k15, M1, k4. (49sts)
Rows 9–14: Change to yarn B and work 6 rows st st.
Rows 15–28: Change to yarn A and work 14 rows g st.
Change to yarn B.
Row 29: K16, [skpo] × 4, k1, [k2tog] × 4, k16. (41sts)
Row 30: K.
Row 31: K10, cast off 21sts, k across remaining 10sts. (This includes 1st after casting off).
Slip first set of 10sts on holder.
Rows 32–34: K.
Row 35: Cast off. Break yarn. Rejoin yarn where you started casting off 21sts. Cast on 13sts.
Row 36: K across cast on sts and 10sts from holder. (23sts)

Row 37 (buttonhole row): K18, k2tog, yfwd, k1. (21sts on needle), turn work.
Row 38: K 21sts on needle.
Cast off all sts.

Left shoe
Work same as for Right shoe to row 31. Put first set of 10sts on holder.
Row 32: K 10sts on needle, turn work and cast on 13sts at end of row.
Row 33: K 23sts.
Row 34 (buttonhole row): K18, yfwd, k2tog, k1. (21sts on needle), turn work.
Row 35: K 21sts on needle.
Cast off all stitches on needle. Rejoin yarn to stitches on holder.
Rows 36–38: K 10sts on needle.
Cast off.

Making up
With WS facing, and using yarn B, sew together rows 9–14 of st st, matching stitch for stitch along the row. This will form a neat seam on the RS of the work. Repeat this on the second shoe. Seam the foot and back of the shoe in a matching colour. Sew buttons on to the shoe to correspond with the buttonholes on the strap.

The pink edging, when sewn together, will form a neat rim for the sole. Ensure that you use a flat seam such as mattress stitch (see p.240) when joining the centre of the sole together to ensure maximum comfort for tiny feet.

Snake scarf

THIS CHILD'S SCARF, WORKED IN MOSS STITCH, is a simple and quick project for someone new to knitting. The cotton yarn is a joy to work with and creates a soft, flat finish. Any DK yarn is suitable for this project, but make sure that you knit a tension square first so that your scarf will be the correct size. Finish your creation with a pom-pom tail (see p.247).

🍃 you will need:

size
15cm x 1.5m (6 x 59in)

materials
Debbie Bliss DK Cotton
50g in
A: Ecru (002) x 2
B: Turquoise (061) x 2
C: Bright red (047) x 1
1 pair of 4mm (UK8/US6) needles
Large-eyed needle

tension
20sts and 30 rows to 10cm (4in) over st st on 4mm (UK8/US6) needles

special abbreviation
MB (make bobble for eye): K into front, back, front, back of st, turn, p4, turn, k4, turn, p4, k2, k2tog, then pass third and fourth sts over first st

🍃 how to make

Striped pattern
Using yarn A, k 10 rows.
Using yarn B, k 6 rows.
Rep throughout, until row 188, then cont in yarn B only.

Body
In yarn A, cast on 2sts.
Row 1: *K1, p1.
Row 2: P1, k1.
Rep from *.
Cont in moss st as above and inc (kfb or pfb) into the first and last st every 4th row. Cont stripe as stated until you are left with 36sts and have 68 rows.
Cont knitting straight in moss st and foll the stripe layout until 177 rows have been knitted.

Rows 178–188: Cont in moss st, dec 1st (k2tog or p2tog) at beg and end of row 178, row 182, and row 188. (30sts)
Rows 189–200: Cont in moss st for 12 rows inc into first and last stitch every 2 rows. (42sts)
Rows 201–225: Cont in moss st straight.
Row 226: Cont in moss st. Dec 1st at beg and end of each row. At sts 17 and 23 MB (in yarn A).
Rows 227–242: Cont in moss st. Dec 1st at beg and end of each row.
Row 243: Change to yarn C. (8sts)
Cont in moss st for 15 rows.

It is easy to tell the difference between the right and wrong sides of your knitting as the joined-in yarn will show up more on the WS.

You can create a pom-pom of any size, but do not make it too large for this project as it will look out of proportion to the snake.

top tip

Make sure that the pom-pom is securely attached to the scarf.

Forked tongue

Row 259: *K1, p1, k1, p1, turn.
Row 260: P1, k1, p1, k1, turn.
Row 261: K1, p1, k1, p1, turn.
Row 262: P1, k1, p1, k1, turn.
Row 263: K1, p1, k1, p1, turn.
Break yarn and cast off these 4sts.
Reattach yarn to rem 4sts and rep from * once more.
Cast off.

Pom-pom

Cut two circles of card (6cm (2½in) diameter); cut a smaller circle out of the centre. Place two circles on top of each other. Wrap yarn C around the circle until there is no hole left in the centre (it is easier to wrap with small bundles of yarn). Using scissors, cut all the way around the edge of the circle, take a separate piece of yarn and wrap it around the middle of the pom-pom, making sure to go between the two pieces of circular card; secure tightly. Remove the card circles and puff up the pom-pom. Sew the pom-pom onto the bottom of the snake as a tail. For more information about making a pom-pom, turn to p.247.

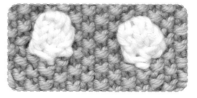

The raised eyes are knitted within the pattern as bobbles. The MB special abbreviation on row 226 uses kfb increases to create 2 stitches from one.

Weave in the yarn tail after casting off to create a neat edge to the forked tongue. (See p.242, Darning in an end, for more information.)

Flower
bobble beanie

A DAISY IN A FIELD OF GRASS – this jolly beanie is decorated with a single flower that is knitted separately and sewn on the hat afterwards; a fun pom-pom tops it off. Worked in stocking stitch, the lower edge of the knitting curls up slightly to create a tiny rim around the hat. Knitted in a bamboo cotton yarn, this beanie can be worn at any time of the year.

you will need

size
To fit a child, aged 0–6 (6–12:12–18:18–24 : 24–36) months

materials
King Cole Bamboo Cotton DK 100g in
A: Green (533) × 1
B: White (530) × 1
C: Yellow (523) × 1
1 pair of 3.25mm (UK10/US3) needles
1 pair of 4mm (UK8/US6) needles
Large-eyed needle

tension
22sts and 30 rows to 10cm (4in) over st st on 4mm (UK8/US6) needles

how to make

Beanie roll edge
Using 3.25mm (UK10/US3) needles and yarn A, cast on 85 (91:97:103: 109) sts using the cable cast on method, working between stitches.
Row 1: K.
Row 2: P.
These 2 rows form st st.
Work a further 4 rows in st st.
Change to 4mm (UK8/US6) needles and beg with a k row, work in st st until hat measures 10 (11:12:13:14) cm (4 (4¼:4¾:5¼:5½)in) from beg, ending with a p row.

Shape the crown
Row 1 (RS): K1, [k2tog, k4] × 14 (15:16:17:18). (71 (76:81:86:91) sts)
Beg with a p row, work 3 rows in st st.
Row 5: K1, [k2tog, k3] × 14 (15:16:17:18). (57 (61:65:69:73) sts)
Beg with a p row, work 3 rows in st st.
Row 9: K1, [k2tog, k2] × 14 (15:16:17:18). (43 (46:49:52:55) sts)
Beg with a p row, work 3 rows in st st.
Row 13: K1, [k2tog, k1] × 14 (15:16: 17:18). (29 (31:33:35:37) sts)
Row 14: P.

Row 15: K1, [k2tog] × 14 (15:16: 17:18). (15 (16:17:18:19) sts)
Row 16: [P2tog] × 7 (8:8:9:9), p1 (0:1:0:1). (8 (8:9:9:10) sts)
Break off yarn leaving a long yarn tail and draw this through rem sts twice, pull up tightly. Use this end to sew the centre back seam using mattress stitch (see p.240), reversing the seam for the last 6 rows and allowing the cast on edge to roll back.

The body of the beanie is knitted in stocking stitch, which causes the edge to curl naturally (see p.215).

To make a perfect, fluffy pom-pom turn to page 247. Sew it on to the hat using yarn C and a large-eyed needle.

Each petal is knitted separately and then joined together before being sewn on top of the hat.

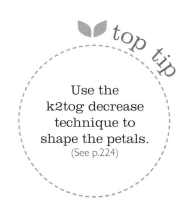

Flower petals

With 4mm (UK8/US6) needles and yarn B, cast on 3sts.
K I row.
Inc 1st at each end of next 2 rows. (7sts)
K I row.
Inc 1st at each end of next row. (9sts)
K 13 rows.
Break yarn and slide the sts of petal down LH needle.
Make 5 more petals in the same way, but don't break yarn on the final petal.

Join the petals

Knit across all of the 6 petals to form the flower as follows:

Row I: [K3, k2tog, k4] × 6. (48sts)
Row 2: [K3, k2tog, k3] × 6. (42sts)
Row 3: [K2, k2tog, k3] × 6. (36sts)
Row 4: [K2, k2tog, k2] × 6. (30sts)
Row 5: [K1, k2tog, k2] × 6. (24sts)
Row 6: [K1, k2tog, k1] × 6. (18sts)
Row 7: [K2tog, k1] × 6. (12sts)
Row 8: [K2tog] × 6. (6sts)
Break off yarn and draw this through rem sts twice, pull up tightly. Use this end to sew the row ends tog to form a flower.

Making up

Sew in all ends. Sew flower to top of hat. Make a medium-sized pom-pom from yarn C (see p.247) and sew this to top of hat in the centre of the flower.

top tip

Use the k2tog decrease technique to shape the petals.
(See p.224)

Classic socks

COLOURFUL AND COMFORTABLE, this pair of socks is stretchy to fit growing feet while cushioning toes and heels as the child runs and plays. Knitted on double-pointed needles – turn to page 237 for detailed information about using this type of needle. If changing the yarn when knitting this project, make sure that you choose a quality that is durable.

❦ you will need

size
To fit a child, aged 0–6 (9–18:24–36) months

materials
Debbie Bliss Baby Cashmerino 50g in
A: Apple (002) × 1
B: Primrose (001) × 1
C: Coral (050) × 1
D: Sky (032) × 1
4 × 3.75mm (UK9/US5) double-pointed needles
Large-eyed needle
Stitch marker

tension
22sts and 28 rows to 10cm (4in) over st st on 3.75mm (UK9/US5) needles

special abbreviation
s1p: Slip one purlwise (see p.218)

❦ how to make

Cuff and ankle (Make 2)
Cast on 25 (29:33) sts in yarn A. Divide the stitches on three of your four needles.
K into first cast on st to form a circle. Place a stitch marker in this stitch to mark the first st of your round.
[K1, p1] for 5 rounds to create a moss stitch cuff. (Odd rows start k1, p1 and even rows start p1, k1.)
Break yarn and join yarn B.
K 12 (14:16) rounds to create the main ankle part of sock.

Heel
Next row: K6 (7:8), turn work. Break yarn B and join yarn C.
Next row: P6 (7:8) sts just knitted then p another 6 (7:8) sts. (12 (14:16) sts)
Rearrange your work over your three needles so that the 12 (14:16) sts in yarn C for the heel are on one needle and the other sts are divided between the two other needles.
On the yarn C heel, work 8 (10:12) rows in st st beg with a k row.
Next row: K7 (9:11), ssk, k1. Turn work, leaving rem 2sts on needle.
Next row: S1p, p3 (5:7), p2tog, p1. Turn, leaving rem 2sts on needle.
Next row: S1p, k4 (6:8), ssk (across

gap), k1.
Next row: S1p, p5 (7:9), p2tog (across gap), p1. (8 (10:12) sts)
Break yarn C.

Foot
With RS of work facing and yarn B, k across 8 (10:12) sts of heel. Remove the stitch marker from the top edge of the cuff and use it to mark the running bar between the 4th and 5th (5th and 6th:6th and 7th) sts you have just knitted to mark the beginning of your round.
Pick up and k5 (6:7) sts up one side of heel.
Turn work and p13 (16:19) sts just worked. With the spare double-pointed needle, pick up and p5 (6:7) sts up the other side of heel.
Turn work and k up to and including st before stitch marker.
You will now have 31 (37:43) sts on your needles.
Starting at the marker, k6 (8:10), k2tog, k15 (17:19), ssk, k to end of round. (29 (35:41) sts)
Next round: K.
Next round: K5 (7:9), k2tog, k15 (17:19), ssk, k to end of round. (27 (33:39) sts)
Next round: K.

top tip

Draw the yarn through the end stitch in the toe to encourage it to curve.

Next round: K4 (6:8), k2tog, k15 (17:19), ssk, k to end of round. (25 (31:37) sts)
Next round: K.
Next round: K3 (5:7), k2tog, k15 (17:19), ssk, k to end of round. (23 (29:35) sts)
Next round: K.
Medium and large sizes only:
Next round: K4 (6), k2tog, k17 (19), ssk, k to end of round. (27 (33) sts)
Next round: K.
Large size only:
Next round: K5, k2tog, k19, ssk, k to end of round. (31sts)
Next round: K.
All sizes:
K 3 (5:7) rounds.
Break yarn B.

Toe
You will now have 23 (27:31) sts on your needles.
Join yarn D.

K 3 rounds.
Next round: K3 (4:5), ssk, k2, k2tog, k5 (7:9), ssk, k2, k2tog, k3 (4:5).
Next round: K.
Next round: K2 (3:4), ssk, k2, k2tog, k3 (5:7), ssk, k2, k2tog, k2 (3:4).
Next round: K.
Next round: K1 (2:3), ssk, k2, k2tog, k1 (3:5), ssk, k2, k2tog, k1 (2:3).
Next round: K.
Medium and large sizes only:
Next round: K1 (2), ssk, k2, k2tog, k1 (3), ssk, k2, k2tog, k1 (2).
All sizes:
Trim yarn and thread tail through rem sts. Pull tightly and secure.

Making up
Weave in all yarn ends. There is no need to block these socks.

The moss stitch cuff helps to "frame" the sock and prevent the top edge from curling. It also helps prevent the sock from falling down.

The heel is both practical and hard-wearing. By slipping stitches, you line the inside of the sock with yarn, making the area more durable.

A rapid decrease around the circular knitted toe creates a smooth and professional finish. Pull the thread tail tightly and weave in.

For *Hooded blanket*

see pages 106–109

Bear-aclava

BALACLAVAS ARE A USEFUL ITEM for cold winter days. This balaclava has two-tone ears for a cute, teddy bear look; however, you can choose to leave the ears off to make a classic style balaclava. We've used a soft, alpaca-rich yarn, but any DK yarn will work well. Smaller needles are used when knitting the ribbing to create a snug-fitting hood around your child's face.

🌱 you will need

size
To fit a child, aged 0–6 (6–12:12–18:18–24:24–36) months

materials
King Cole Baby Alpaca DK 50g in
A: Camel (500) × 2
B: Koala (504) × 1
1 pair of 3.25mm (UK10/US3) needles
1 pair of 4mm (UK8/US6) needles
2 safety pins
Stitch holder

tension
22sts and 28 rows to 10cm (4in) over st st on 4mm (UK8/US6) needles

special instruction
cable cast on: Work as Knit-on cast on (see p.208), but after the second stitch is made, insert needle between last two stitches to make each new one

🌱 how to make

Ribbed neck and hood
Using 3.25mm (UK10/US3) needles and yarn A, cast on 69 (73:77:77:81) sts using the cable cast on method.
Row 1: P1, *k1, p1, rep from * to end.
Row 2: K1, *p1, k1, rep from * to end.
These 2 rows form 1x1 rib.
Work a further 15 (15:17:17:19) rows in 1x1 rib.
Next row: Rib 8sts then slip these sts onto a safety pin, rib 5 (4:3:3:2) sts, inc in next st, [rib 6 (7:8:8:9) sts, inc in next st] × 6, rib 5 (4:3:3:2), s last 8sts on LH needle onto a safety pin. (60 (64:68:68:72) sts)
Change to 4mm (UK8/US6) needles and beg with a k row, work in st st until hood measures 18 (20:22:5: 22.5:24.5)cm (7 (8:9:9:9½)in) from beg ending with a p row.

Shape top
Next row: K39 (41:44:44:47) sts, k2tog tbl, turn.
Next row: S1p, p18 (18:20:20:22) sts, p2tog, turn.
Next row: S1p, k18 (18:20:20:22) sts, k2tog tbl, turn.
Rep the last 2 rows until all sts are dec on each side of centre sts, ending with a p row.

The evenly shaped crown uses the purl two together (p2tog, see p.225) decrease and the knit two together (k2tog, see p.224) decrease. K2tog is worked through the back of the loops (see p.218).

Attach the inner ears to the piece of outer knitting using invisible mattress stitch (see p.240) to create the two-tone ears.

Leave rem 20 (20:22:22:24) sts on a stitch holder.

Work edging
With RS facing and 3.25mm (UK10/US3) needles, join yarn B and rib across 8sts on safety pin, pick up and k29 (32:36:36:39) sts up RS of hood, k across 20 (20:22:22:24) sts on holder dec 1st at centre, pick up and k29 (32:36:36:39) sts down LS of hood, then rib 8sts on safety pin. (93 (99:109:109:117) sts)
Work 5 rows in 1x1 rib as set.
Cast off evenly in rib.

Outer ears (Make 4)
Using 4mm (UK8/US6) needles and yarn A, cast on 16sts.
Beg with a k row, work 8 rows in st st.
Dec 1st at each end of next and foll

2 alt rows. (10sts)
P 1 row.
Cast off.

Inner ears (Make 2)
Using 4mm (UK8/US6) needles and yarn B cast on 12sts.
K 6 rows.
Dec 1st at each end of next and foll alt row. (8sts)
Cast off.

Making up
Sew in all ends. Sew centre front chin seam. With RS facing, sew each pair of outer ears together, leaving the bottom edge open. Turn RS out and oversew the cast on edges together. Sew an inner ear to each outer ear and then sew to sides of balaclava in positions as shown.

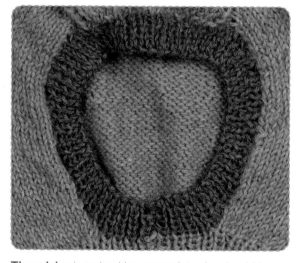

The edging is made with a contrasting colour by picking up stitches from the hood section and working 5 rows of 1 x 1 ribbing. The ribbing gives the edge an almost elastic fit.

The neck section is worked in rib for a warm, snug fit. Join the seam under the chin using mattress stitch, making sure to evenly match both sides of the knitted fabric as you go.

Flower headband

THIS FLOWER HEADBAND WILL KEEP HAIR out of your little one's eyes, or just act as a pretty accessory. It's so simple to knit you can have it completed in just a few hours. The flower-centre button can be left off the finished headband if you want a completely soft headband suitable for young babies.

how to make

Headband
Cast on 9sts in yarn A.
Row 1: K2, [yfwd, k2tog] × 3, k1.
Next row: P2, k5, p2.
K 2 rows.
Rep last 4 rows × 27 (29:31).
Cast off.

Outer flower petals
Cast on 10sts in yarn B.
Row 1: [Inc 1st] × 2.
Turn and work on 4sts just knitted.
Work 9 rows in st st beg with a p row.
Next row: K2tog, ssk. Lift first st on needle over second st. (1st)
*Next row: K1 into next cast on st, inc 1st.
Turn and work on 4sts on needle only.
Work 9 rows in st st beg with a p row.
Next row: K2tog, ssk. Lift first st on needle over second st.** (1st)
Rep from * to ** × 3.
K into first cast on st to complete final petal. (2sts)
Cast off 1st. Break yarn and pull it through rem st.

Inner flower petals
Cast on 10sts in yarn B.
Row 1: [Inc 1st] × 2.

Turn and work on 4sts just knitted.
Work 5 rows in st st beg with a p row.
Next row: K2tog, ssk. Lift first st on needle over second st. (1st)
*Next row: K1 into next cast on st, inc 1st.
Turn and work on 4sts on needle.
Work 5 rows in st st beg with a p row.
Next row: K2tog, ssk. Lift first st on needle over second st.** (1st)
Rep from * to ** × 3.
K into first cast on st to complete final petal. (2sts)
Cast off 1st. Break yarn and pull it through rem st.

Making up
Seam the two short ends of the headband together using mattress stitch (see p.240).

Join both the outer and inner petals into a circle. Place the inner petals onto the outer petals so that each inner petal lies between two outer petals. Secure the flower in place on the headband and stitch the button to the flower centre with cream sewing thread.

Practise your increase and decrease skills (see pp.220–227) to knit the undulating flower petals in this pretty two-tiered bloom.

🌿 **you will need**

- -

size
To fit a child, aged 0–6 (9–12:
12–36) months

materials
Sublime Baby Cashmerino Silk
DK 50g in
A: Gooseberry (004) × 1
B: Cheeky (048) × 1
1 pair of 3.75mm (UK9/US5)
needles

Large-eyed needle
Sewing needle
Cream sewing thread
1 × 16mm (¾in) mother-of-pearl
button

tension
23sts and 40 rows to 10cm (4in)
over lace st on 3.75mm (UK9/
US5) needles

Striped mittens

THESE CHUNKY LITTLE MITTENS are quick to make and use only two simple shaping techniques. The ribbing gives an elasticated and comfortable cuff, while a knitted i-cord means that the mittens will stay safely within your child's coat rather than getting dropped on the ground.

🌿 you will need

size
Ages 18–36 months

materials
Rowan Pure Wool DK 50g in
A: Indigo (010) × 1
B: Cypress (007) × 1
C: Pier (006) × 1
1 pair of 4mm (UK8/US6) needles
1 pair of 3.75mm (UK9/US5) needles
4 × 4mm (UK8/US6) double-pointed needles

tension
22sts and 30 rows to 10cm (4in) over st st on 4mm (UK8/US6) needles

🌱 how to make

Right mitt

With 3.75mm (UK9/US5) needles and yarn A, cast on 26sts.
Work 8 rows of 1×1 rib, [k1, p1] to end.
Change to 4mm (UK8/US6) needles.

Stripe sequence

Work 2 rows in yarn B, 2 rows in yarn A. Rep x 4.
Work 2 rows in yarn B, 2 rows in yarn C. Rep x 3.
Work 2 rows in yarn B, 1 row in yarn C.
Cast off in yarn C.
Foll stripe sequence while working the mitt as described below. Cont the stripe sequence on the thumb, finishing on the second stripe in yarn C.
Work 4 rows st st, starting with a k row.

Right thumb gusset

Row 1: K13, kfb, kfb, k to end.
Rows 2, 4, and 6: P to end.
Row 3: K13, kfb, k2, kfb, k to end.
Row 5: K13, kfb, k4, kfb, k to end.
Cont inc in this way until there are 34sts on the needle, finishing with a p row.

Right thumb

Next row: K23, turn, cast on 1st, p11 (which includes cast on st), turn, cast on 1st. (12sts)
Working on these 12sts, cont in st st for 12 rows. Thread yarn through and fasten off.
Sew up thumb seam.
With RS facing and working from last st on RH needle, pick up 2sts at base of thumb and k across LH needle.
Next row: P to end.
Cont in st st for 12 rows.

Shape the top

Row 1: K1, k2tog in back of st, k7, k2tog, k2, k2tog in back of st, k to last 3sts, k2tog, k1.
Row 2 and 4: P to end.
Row 3: K1, k2tog in back of st, k5, k2tog, k2, k2tog in back of st, k to last 3sts, k2tog, k1.
Row 5: K1, k2tog in back of st, k3, k2tog, k2, k2tog in back of st, k to last 3sts, k2tog, k1.
Cast off purlwise.

Left mitt

Work as for Right mitt up to Right thumb gusset.

Left thumb gusset

Row 1: K11, kfb, kfb, k to end.
Rows 2, 4, and 6: P to end.
Row 3: K11, kfb, k2, kfb, k to end.
Row 5: K11, kfb, k4, kfb, k to end.

Cont inc in this way until there are 34sts on the needle, finishing with a p row.

Left thumb

Next row: K21, turn, cast on 1st, p11 (which includes cast on st), turn, cast on 1st. (12sts)
Working on these 12sts, finish Thumb and rest of mitt as for Right mitt.

I-cord

With 4mm (UK8/US6) double-pointed needles and yarn A, cast on 3sts.
*K3, do not turn work, slide to right end of needle, pull yarn around back of sts to tighten.
Rep from * until the cord measures two and half times the length of one of the child's arms (see p.229).

Making up

Sew top and side seams taking care to match the stripes. Stitch i-cord in place at inside top edge of rib above thumbs.

Pull the yarn firmly along the back of your knitted stitches to create a neat, tight cord.

The kfb increases (see p.219) on the thumb gusset should not leave any holes or uneven stitches.

This tiny bonnet sits against the baby's head, holding its shape with soft ribbing that is just snug enough to retain warmth.

Newborn hat

THIS QUICK AND EASY HAT IS DESIGNED TO MATCH the Newborn cardigan on pages 26–29 and Newborn booties on pages 194–195. It is sized to fit a newborn baby, but can be made bigger by using a thicker yarn with the appropriate needles. For example, try a different DK yarn with 4mm (UK8/US6) needles to make a hat for a baby aged three to six months.

🍃 you will need

size
To fit a newborn baby

materials
Rowan cashsoft DK 50g in Sky pink (540) × 1
1 pair of 3.25mm (UK10/US3) needles
Large-eyed needle

tension
25sts and 34 rows to 10cm (4in) over st st on 3.25mm (UK10/US3) needles

special abbreviations
rib: Work in rib, knitting all presented k sts and purling all presented p sts
rib2tog: Working in rib, k2tog

🍃 how to make

Pattern
Cast on 83sts using the cable cast on method.
Row 1 (RS): *K1, p1, rep from * to last st, k1.
Row 2: *P1, k1, rep from * to last st, p1.
Rep last 2 rows once more.
Row 5: [Rib 13, rib2tog] × 5, rib to end. (78sts)
Next row: P.
Next row: K.
These 2 rows form st st.
Work in st st for a further 17 rows.

Shape crown
Row 1 (RS): [K6, k2tog] × 9, k to end. (69sts)
Row 2 and every foll alt row: P.
Row 3: K.
Row 5: [K5, k2tog] × 9, k to end. (60sts)
Row 7: [K4, k2tog] × 9, k to end. (51sts)
Row 9: [K3, k2tog] × 10, k to end. (41sts)
Row 11: [K2, k2tog] × 10, k to end. (31sts)
Row 13: [K1, k2tog] × 10, k to end. (21sts)
Row 15: [K2tog] × 10, k1. (11sts)

Break off yarn, leaving a long yarn tail and draw this through rem sts twice. Use this end to join the back seam with mattress stitch (see p.240). Steam block lightly.

By tightly pulling the yarn through the stitches twice at the top of the hat, you will prevent gaps from forming in the future.

Snuggly slippers

THESE CUTE SLIPPERS are perfect for keeping little feet warm around the house. They are quick to knit – three sections worked in chunky-weight yarn – and take just over one ball of wool, so are great value for money. The slippers will be very slippery on hard floors, but are perfect for floors with carpeting.

🍃 you will need

size
To fit a child, aged 1–3 years

materials
Sublime Cashmere Merino Silk Aran 50g in Regatta (138) x 2
1 pair of 4mm (UK8/US6) needles
Large-eyed needle

tension
18sts and 24 rows to 10cm (4in) over g st on 4mm (UK8/US6) needles

special abbreviation
MB (make bobble): Kfb, turn, p3, turn, skpo

🍃 how to make

Back section
Cast on 2sts.
Row 1: K to end.
Row 2: Kfb, k1.
*Rows 3 and 4: K to end.
Row 5: Kfb, k to end.*
Rep from * to * inc in this way by adding 1st on alt ends until there are 10sts on the needle. Cast on 18sts.
Next row: K18, p1, k8, p1, cast on 18sts. (46sts)

Middle section
Row 1: K5, p1, k to last 6sts, p1, k5.
Row 2: K1, MB, k16, p1, k8, p1, k to end.
Row 3: K5, p1, k to last 6sts, p1, k5.
Row 4: K18, p1, k8, p1, k to last 2sts, MB, k1.
Rep rows 1–4 x 6.
Next row: Cast off 9sts, k to last 6sts, p1, k5.

Toe section
Row 1: Cast off 9sts leaving 1st on RH needle, [p1, k1] x 4, p1, k8, [p1, k1] x 5. (28sts)
Row 2: [P1, k1] x 5, k8, [k1, p1] x 5.
Row 3: [K1, p1] x 5, k8, [p1, k1] x 5.
Rep rows 2–3 x 7.
Next row: K2tog to end.
Next row: P to end.
Next row: K2tog to end.
Thread yarn through remaining 7sts and secure.

Making up
Sew side edges together along ribbing to make toe then continue sewing cast off edges together to form fold-over top. Sew side edges of back triangle to cast on sts of sides then continue sewing cast on edges together to form fold-over top.

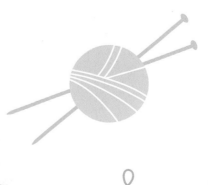

The shaped heel and back of the slipper is created using the knit 1 front and back (kfb) increase method (see p.219).

Use mattress stitch (see p.240) to sew the seams that form the slipper shape together. Work the stitches loosely in order not to misshape the knitted fabric.

Create the tiny knitted bobbles using the sl k1 psso (skpo) decrease method (see p.225).

Cast off loosely before knitting the ribbed toe section so the stitches sit neatly against each other.

For *Cosy hoodie* see pages 54–57

Beanie
with ears

AN ADORABLE HAT with two dainty ears is fun to wear and simple to knit – worked in stocking stitch and edged with a 1×1 ribbed border, the edge stretches gently for a comfortable fit. The ears are knitted separately and then easily sewn on with a blunt-ended needle.

top tip

Have fun with colour. Choose contrasting yarns for the hat and ears.

🌱 you will need

size
To fit a child, aged 0–6 (6–12:
12–18:18–24) months
Actual measurements:
Circumference
42 (45:47:49)cm
(16½ (17¾:18½:19½)in)

materials
King Cole Magnum Chunky
100g in
Aqua (348) × 1
1 pair of 6mm (UK4/US10)
needles
Blunt-ended needle

tension
14sts and 20 rows to 10cm
(4in) over st st on 6mm
(UK4/US10) needles

🌱 how to make

Ribbed edging
Cast on 58 (62:66:68) sts using the
cable cast on method, working
between stitches.

Rib row: *K1, p1, rep from * to end.
This row forms rib.
Work another 3 rows in rib.
Next row: K.
Next row: P.
These 2 rows form st st.
Work in st st until hat measures
9.5 (10.5:11.5:12.5)cm (3¾ (4¼:
4½:5)in) from beg, ending with a
p row.

Shape the crown
Row 1 (RS): K4 (2:5:1), k2tog, [k5
(5:4:5), k2tog] × 7 (8:9:9), k3 (2:5:2).
(50 (53:56:58) sts)
Row 2 and every foll alt row: P.
Row 3: K3 (1:4:1), k2tog, [k4 (4:3:4),
k2tog] × 7 (8:9:9), k3 (2:5:1).
(42 (44:46:48) sts)
Row 5: K2 (1:4:1), k2tog, [k3 (3:2:3),
k2tog] × 7 (8:9:9), k3 (1:4:0).
(34 (35:36:38) sts)
Row 7: K2 (1:3:0), k2tog, [k2 (2:1:2),
k2tog] × 7 (8:9:9), k2 (0:4:0).
(26 (26:26:28) sts)
Row 9: *K2tog, rep from * to end.
(13 (13:13:14) sts)
Row 10: *P2tog, rep from * to last
1 (1:1:0) st, p1 (1:1:0). (7 (7:7:7) sts)
Row 11: [K2tog] × 3, k1. (4 (4:4:4) sts)

Break off yarn leaving a long yarn tail
and draw this through rem sts twice;

Shape the rounded teddy bear
ears by increasing and decreasing the
stitches using skpo and k2tog. The
stocking stitch causes them to curl.

pull up tightly. Use this end to sew the
centre back seam using mattress stitch
(see p.240).

Ears
Cast on 7sts.
Beg with a k row, work 4 rows in
st st.
Next row: Skpo, k3, k2tog. (5sts)
P 1 row.
Cast off.

Making up
Stitch the ears to the hat, in the
positions as shown, using a blunt-
ended needle and yarn.

Floral beanie

A PRETTY, LOOSE-FITTING HAT FOR A GIRL, which is knitted with a zigzag eyelet stitch above the rib and decorated with flowers that feature a French knot in the centre. Try knitting the hat with smaller-sized needles and a thinner yarn to make a hat for a younger baby, or use larger needles and a thicker yarn for an older child.

🌿 you will need

size
To fit a child, aged 2–3 years

materials
Debbie Bliss Cotton DK
50g in
Coral (064) × 1
Scrap of yarn for French knot
(we've used White (001))
1 pair of 3.25mm (UK10/
US3) needles
1 pair of 3.75mm (UK9/US5)
needles
Large-eyed needle

tension
22sts and 30 rows to 10cm
(4in) over st st on 3.75mm
(UK9/US5) needles

special abbreviations
MB (make bobble): K1, p1
in the next st. Turn, p2.
Turn, skpo

🌿 how to make

With 3.25mm (UK10/US3) needles,
cast on 98sts.

Ribbed edging
Rows 1–6: [K1, p1] to end.
Change to 3.75mm (UK9/US5)
needles.

Zigzag eyelet
Row 7: K1, [yrn, k2tog, k2] to last
st, k1.
Rows 8, 10, and 12: P to end.
Row 9: K1, [k2, yrn, k2tog] to last
st, k1.
Row 11: K to end.

Flower design (Embroidered knot centre)
Row 1: [K5, MB, k1, MB] to last
2sts, k2.
Row 2 and all even rows: P to end.
Row 3: K1, [k3, MB], to last st, k1.
Row 5: Rep row 1.
Row 7: K to end.

Flower design (Eyelet centre)
Row 9: K1, [MB, k1, MB, k5] to last
st, k1.
Row 11: K1, [k1, yrn, k2tog, MB, k3,

MB] to last st, k1.
Row 13: Rep row 9.
Row 15: K to end.
Row 17: [K5, MB, k1, MB] to last
2sts, k2.
Row 19: K1, [k3, MB, k1, yrn, k2tog,
MB] to last st, k1.
Row 21: Rep row 17.
Row 22: P to end.

Shape crown
Row 1: [Skpo, k1, k2tog, k3] to last
2sts, k2. (74sts)
Row 2 and all even rows: P to end.

🌿 top tip
Make a few
practice bobbles
before you
start knitting
the hat.

Row 3: K2, MB, [k3, MB, k1, MB] to last 5sts, k3, MB, k1.

Row 5: K1, yrn, k2tog, MB, [k1, MB, k1, yrn, k2tog, MB] to last 4sts, k1, MB, k2.

Row 7: As row 3.

Row 9: K2, k2tog, [k1, skpo, k1, k2tog] to last 4sts, k1, skpo, k1. (50sts)

Row 11: K1, [yon, k2tog, k2] to last st, k1.

Row 13: K1, [k2, yon, k2tog] to last st, k1.

Row 15: K1, [k2tog, k2] to last st, k1. (38sts)

Row 17: K1, [k2tog, k1] to last st, k1. (26sts)

Row 19: K1, [k2tog] to last st, k1. (14sts)

Row 21: K1, [k2tog] to last st, k1. (8sts)

Cut yarn and thread through rem sts, draw up tightly and secure.

Making up

Embroider a French knot at the centre of each of the first row of flowers in a contrasting yarn.

To make a French knot, knot the end of a strand of yarn and bring it out where the knot is wanted. Wrap the thread twice around the needle. Pull the wraps tight against the fabric and insert the needle back next to its starting point. Hold the knot against the fabric and take the thread through to the back. Secure it with a small backstitch. Sew back seam, 1st in from the edge.

The combination of raised bobble "petals" and an open eyelet centre gives each flower an eye-catching pronounced texture.

The textured design continues right up to the crown of the beanie where the rows of eyelets form a decorative circle.

French knots at the centre of the first row of flowers add a light touch of a contrasting colour. A ribbed edge stretches to fit comfortably.

top tip

The seams along
the base of the
booties sit flat
for comfort.

The fold-down cuff is knitted
as one long piece, then folded
and stitched to create a casing
for the ribbon. The cast off
adds a wavy edge.

Newborn booties

THESE TINY BOOTIES CURVE GENTLY to follow the shape of a baby's foot, providing plenty of room for growth. Increases and decreases curve the booties as you knit. We've chosen a soft DK yarn and used smaller than usually recommended needles to achieve a firm fabric suitable for keeping tiny toes warm and protected.

🌱 you will need

size
To fit a newborn baby

materials
Rowan Cashsoft Baby DK 50g in
Sky pink (540) x 1
1 pair of 3mm (UK11/USn/a) needles
1 pair of 2.75mm (UK12/US2) needles
70cm (27½in) co-ordinating ribbon, 3–7mm (⅛–⅜in) wide
Large-eyed needle

tension
25sts and 46 rows to 10cm (4in) over g st on 3mm (UK11/USn/a) needles

🌱 how to make

Booties (Make 2)
Using 3mm (UK11/USn/a) needles, cast on 37sts.
Row 1 (WS): K.
Row 2: Inc in next st, k15, inc in next st, k3, inc in next st, k15, inc in last st. (41sts)
Rows 3, 5, and 7: K.
Row 4: Inc in next st, k17, inc in next st, k3, inc in next st, k17, inc in last st. (45sts)
Row 6: Inc in next st, k19, inc in next st, k3, inc in next st, k19, inc in last st. (49sts)
K 16 rows, ending with a WS row.

Shape for toe
Row 1 (RS): K17, skpo, k11, k2tog, k17. (47sts)
Row 2: K17, skpo, k9, k2tog, k17. (45sts)
Row 3: K17, skpo, k7, k2tog, k17. (43sts)
Row 4: K17, skpo, k5, k2tog, k17. (41sts)
Row 5: K17, skpo, k3, k2tog, k17. (39sts)
Row 6: K17, skpo, k1, k2tog, k17. (37sts)
Row 7: K17, sk2p, k17. (35sts)

Shape for ankle
Change to 2.75mm (UK12/US2) needles and work as follows:
Next row (RS): K1, *p1, k1, rep from * to end.
Next row: P1, *k1, p1, rep from * to end.
Rep last 2 rows x 2.
Eyelet row: K1, *yon, k2tog, rep from * to end.
Next row: P1, *k1, p1, rep from * to end.

Work edging
Next row: (Casting off) *k2, pass first st over second so that 1st rem on RH needle as if casting off, place this 1st back on LH needle, rep from * until 1st remains.

Making up
Fasten off, leaving a long yarn tail. Join row ends with mattress stitch (see p.240) using the yarn tail from cast off edge. Fold over ribbed edging and catch to main bootie with a long running stitch. Thread ribbon through eyelets and tie in a bow. Sew a few stitches through the yarn and ribbon to prevent the ribbon coming undone.

Scarf hat

WORKED IN STOCKING STITCH, this adorable scarf hat makes a speedy project that's perfect to knit just before a cold snap sets in. Check your tension as you knit to maintain an even pattern across the hat and two scarves. Turn to page 247 to make the pom-poms, making sure that you don't make them too big or they may weigh down and distort the knitting.

🌿 you will need

size
To fit a child, aged 0–6 (6–12:12–18:18–24: 24–36) months

materials
King Cole Merino Blend Chunky 50g in
A: Mint (922) × 3 (3:3:4:4)
B: Cream (919) × 2 (2:2:2:2)
1 pair of 6mm (UK4/US10) needles
Spare needle of the same size

tension
14sts and 26 rows to 10cm (4in) over g st on 6mm (UK4/US10) needles

special instruction
cable cast on: Work as Knit-on cast on (see p.208), but after the second stitch is made, insert needle between last two stitches to make each new one

🌿 how to make

Scarf (Make 2)
Using yarn A, cast on 14 (15:15: 17:17) sts using the cable cast on method.
Work in g st until scarf measures 31 (35:41.5:42.5:43.5)cm (12¼ (14:16¼: 16½:17)in) from beg, ending with a WS row (even row).
Leave sts on a spare needle.

Hat
Using yarn A, cast on 2 (2:3:3:4) sts using the cable cast on method, break yarn. With RS facing, s14 (15:15: 17:17) sts of one scarf onto LH needle next to cast on sts, rejoin yarn and cast on 22 (24:25:26:26) sts using the cable cast on method, break yarn, then s14 (15:15:17:17) sts of other scarf onto LH needle, rejoin yarn and cast on 2 (2:3:3:4) sts using the cable cast on method. (54 (58:61:66:68) sts)
Work in g st until hat measures 16 (17:18:19:20)cm (6¼ (6¾:7:7½:8)in) from cast on sts ending with a WS row.
Cast off fairly loosely.

Making up
Sew in all ends. Sew centre back seam of hat. Flatten hat so that the seam is at centre back between the two scarves, sew across the top edges to join.

Make two large pom-poms in yarn B (see p.247), then four smaller pom-poms. Sew each of the large pom-poms to the top corners of the hat, then sew each of the smaller pom-poms to the bottom corners of each scarf (see photograph, right).

Work each stitch of the seams through the pips formed along the edges of the knitting. On the RS, the seam will not show.

top tip

Cable cast on makes a substantial edge on the hat and scarf.

Knit a *nursery of best friends,* see pages 68–103

Tools and techniques

Yarns

In its simplest form, yarn is made from combed fibres spun together for strength and durability. There are, however, numerous fibre mixes, textures, and effect yarns now available offering exciting creative possibilities to the hand knitter.

yarn weights

Yarns come in many different weights and thicknesses, which affect the appearance of an item and the number of stitches required to knit a sample tension square of 10cm (4in). Find the most suitable weight of yarn, according to project, below. The yarn weight names give the common UK term(s) first, followed by the US term(s).

❧ Yarn weight chart

What do you want to knit?	Yarn weight	Yarn symbol	Recommended needle sizes		
			EU Metric	Old UK	US
Lace	Lace, 2-ply, fingering	**0** Lace	2mm 2.5mm	14 13	0 1
Fine-knit socks, shawls, babywear	Superfine, 3-ply, fingering, baby	**1** Superfine	2.75mm 3mm 3.25mm	12 11 10	2 N/A 3
Light jumpers, babywear, socks, accessories	Fine, 4-ply, sport, baby	**2** Fine	3.5mm 3.75mm 4mm	N/A 9 8	4 5 6
Jumpers, light-weight scarves, blankets, toys	Double-knit (DK), light worsted, 5–6-ply	**3** Light	4.5mm	7	7
Jumpers, cabled menswear, blankets, hats, scarves, mittens	Aran, medium, worsted, Afghan, 12-ply	**4** Medium	5mm 5.5mm	6 5	8 9
Rugs, jackets, blankets, hats, legwarmers, winter accessories	Bulky, chunky, craft, rug, 14-ply	**5** Bulky	6mm 6.5mm 7mm 8mm	4 3 2 0	10 10½ N/A 11
Heavy blankets, rugs, thick scarves	Super bulky, super chunky, bulky, roving, 16-ply and upwards	**6** Super Bulky	9mm 10mm	00 000	13 15

yarn labels

Everything you need to know about a yarn is on its label, represented by a symbol. Always keep the labels as they are vital for identifying the yarn if you run short and need more. New yarn needs to have the same dye lot number as the original purchase in order to avoid a slight difference in colour in the finished item.

Symbols

Yarn manufacturers may use a system of symbols to give details of a yarn. These include descriptions of suitable needles and the required tension.

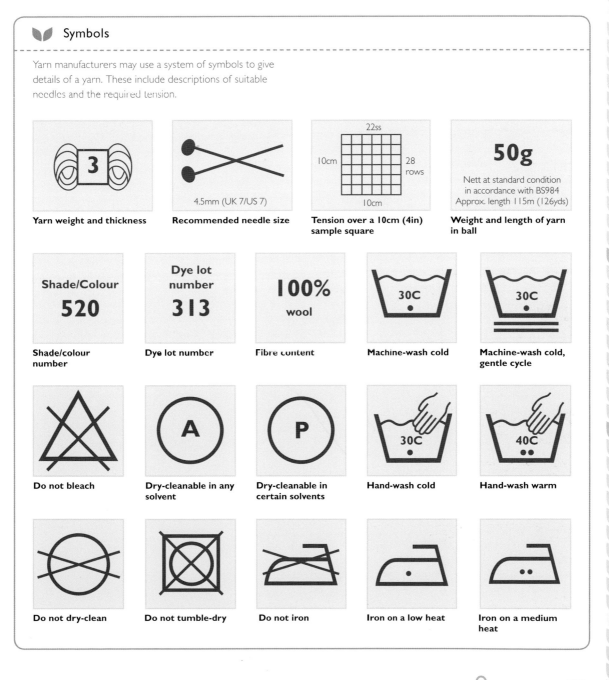

Yarn weight and thickness

Recommended needle size
4.5mm (UK 7/US 7)

Tension over a 10cm (4in) sample square
22ss — 10cm — 28 rows — 10cm

Weight and length of yarn in ball
50g
Nett at standard condition in accordance with BS984
Approx. length 115m (126yds)

Shade/colour number
Shade/Colour 520

Dye lot number
Dye lot number 313

Fibre content
100% wool

Machine-wash cold
30C

Machine-wash cold, gentle cycle
30C

Do not bleach

Dry-cleanable in any solvent
A

Dry-cleanable in certain solvents
P

Hand-wash cold
30C

Hand-wash warm
40C

Do not dry-clean

Do not tumble-dry

Do not iron

Iron on a low heat

Iron on a medium heat

Knitting needles

Needles come in assorted types and are made of different materials, with various benefits when using particular techniques or working with certain fibres. Discover here how to choose the most suitable needles for the project you have in mind.

straight needles

Straight needles give a great deal of support to the hand when knitting. If you are new to knitting, start with these. Short needles are recommended for small projects; long needles are more suitable for wider knits, such as a baby's blanket, and for knitters who like to work by holding the needles underneath their arms.

Metal needles

When working with hairy fibres that may stick, slippery metal needles are great. If you find that you tend to knit too tightly, the slippery surface can help as it will cause a knitter's tension to loosen. Needles of more than 8mm (UK0/US11) in diameter can be clunky to work with, so are rarely available.

Bamboo needles

Bamboo is a lightweight, flexible material, and makes excellent knitting needles. It helps to keep stitches regularly spaced, creating an even knitted fabric with a good tension. Great for slippery fibres such as silk, mercerized cotton, and bamboo yarn. Recommended for arthritis sufferers. Thin needles will gradually warp with use to fit the curvature of your hand.

Plastic needles

For needles with a surface that is halfway between that of metal and that of bamboo, choose plastic. Plastic remains at a steady temperature during use, which may suit people who have arthritis. Avoid plastic needles of 4mm (UK8/US6) or smaller, as heavy projects may bend or break them.

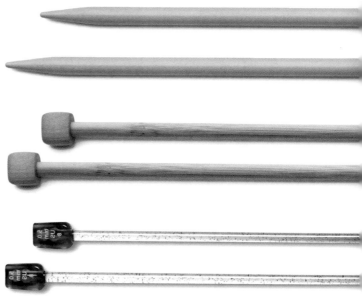

circular needles

A flexible tube joins two needles to make a pair of circular needles. These come in different lengths and thicknesses. Choose a length that is most appropriate for your project: it should match the anticipated diameter of the knitted tube. For instance, a hat would call for shorter circular needles than a jumper knitted in this way. Knitting patterns usually specify the size required for the project.

double-pointed needles

The recommended option for socks, gloves, and narrow tubes. These needles are short and do not accommodate a large number of stitches. At first, some knitters may find that ladders form on each corner between the needles; however, this problem will disappear as you practise.

Conversion chart

This chart gives the closest equivalents between the three needle-sizing systems. The sizes don't match exactly in many cases, but are the nearest equivalents.

EU Metric	Old UK	US
1.5mm	N/A	000 00
2mm	14	0
2.25mm 2.5mm	13	1
2.75mm	12	2
3mm	11	N/A
3.25mm	10	3
3.5mm	N/A	4
3.75mm	9	5
4mm	8	6
4.5mm	7	7
5mm	6	8
5.5mm	5	9
6mm	4	10
6.5mm	3	10½
7mm	2	N/A
7.5mm	1	N/A
8mm	0	11
9mm	00	13
10mm	000	15
12mm	N/A	17
15mm	N/A	19
20mm	N/A	35
25mm	N/A	50

needle size

Knitting needles vary in diameter, from 1.5mm (¹⁄₁₆in) to over 25mm (1in). There are three common sizing systems: European metric, old British sizes, and American sizes. The chart, right, shows you how to convert between these systems. Needles are also available in various lengths to suit different projects.

Following patterns

Stitch pattern instructions are written or charted directions for working both coloured and textured knitting. Patterns can look daunting at first, but if approached step by step they are easy to understand. The following information can help if you get stuck.

understanding written instructions

Anyone who can cast on, knit and purl, and cast off will be able to work from simple knit-and-purl-combination stitch pattern instructions. It is just a question of following the instructions and getting used to the abbreviations. A list of common knitting abbreviations is given below, but for simple knit and purl textures all you need to grasp is that "k1" means "knit one stitch", "k2" means "knit two stitches", and so on. The same applies for purl stitches – "p1" means "purl one stitch", "p2" means "purl two stitches", and so on.

To begin a stitch pattern, cast on the number of stitches that it tells you to, using your chosen yarn and the recommended needles. Follow the pattern and work the stitches row by row and the pattern will grow beneath the needles.

The best tips for first-timers are to follow the rows slowly; mark the right side of the fabric by knotting a coloured thread onto it; use a row counter to keep track of where you are; and pull out your stitches and start again if you get in a muddle.

Knitting abbreviations

These are the most frequently used knitting abbreviations. Any special abbreviations in knitting instructions are always explained within the pattern.

alt	alternate	**p**	purl	**s2 k1 p2sso**	slip 2, knit one, pass
beg	begin(ning)	**p2tog**	purl next 2sts		slipped stitches over
cm	centimetre(s)	**(or dec 1)**	together (see p.225)		(see p.227)
cont	continu(e)(ing)	**patt**	pattern, or work in	**st(s)**	stitch(es)
dec	decreas(e)(ing)		pattern	**st st**	stocking stitch
foll	follow(s)(ing)	**pfb (or inc 1)**	purl into front and	**tbl**	through back of
g	gram(s)		back of next st		loop(s)
g st	garter stitch		(see p.219)	**tog**	together
in	inch(es)	**psso**	pass slipped stitch over	**WS**	wrong side (of work)
inc	increas(e)(ing)	**rem**	remain(s)(ing)	**yd**	yard(s)
k	knit	**rep**	repeat(ing)	**yfwd**	yarn forward (US yo;
k1 tbl	knit st through back	**rev st st**	reverse stocking stitch		see p.222)
	of loop	**RH**	right hand	**yfrn**	yarn forward round
k2tog	knit next 2sts	**RS**	right side (of work)		needle (US yo;
(or dec 1)	together (see p.224)	**sl k1 psso**	slip one, knit one,		see p.223)
kfb	knit into front and	**(skpo)**	pass slipped st	**yo**	yarn over needle
(or inc 1)	back of next st		over (see p.225)		(see p.223)
	(see p.219)	**sl k2tog psso**	slip one st, knit 2sts	**yrn**	yarn round needle
LH	left hand	**(or sk2p)**	together, pass slipped sts		(US yo; see p.222)
m	metre(s)		over (see p.227)	**[ ] ***	repeat instructions
M1 (or M1k)	make one stitch	**ssk**	slip, slip, knit		between brackets, or
	(see p.220)		(see p.226)		after or between asterisks,
mm	millimetre(s)	**s**	slip stitch(es)		as many times as instructed
oz	ounce(s)				

understanding stitch symbols and charts

As well as being written as abbreviations, for example "yo" or "sk2p" as shown opposite, stitch manipulations may be represented symbolically. Stitch symbols, usually laid out in chart form, are particularly helpful for understanding complex stitch manipulations such as lace and cables.

Stitch symbols

These are some of the commonly used knitting symbols. Any unusual symbols will be explained in the pattern. Symbols can vary, so follow the explanations in your pattern.

☐ = k on RS rows, p on WS rows
⊡ = p on RS rows, k on WS rows
⊙ = yarnover (see p.222)
☑ = k2tog (see p.224)
☒ = ssk (see p.226)
☒ = sk2p (see p.227)
☒ = s2 k1 p2sso (see p.227)

Charts

Knitting instructions for stitch patterns can also be given in chart form. Some knitters prefer working stitch-symbol charts because they are easy to read, and they build up a visual image of the stitch repeat that is quick to memorize.

Even with charted instructions, there are usually written directions for how many stitches to cast on. If not, you can calculate the cast on from the chart, where the number of stitches in the pattern "repeat" are clearly marked. Cast on a multiple of this number, plus any edge stitches outside the repeat.

Each square represents a stitch and each horizontal line of squares represents a row. After casting on, work from the bottom of the chart upwards. Read odd-numbered rows (usually RS rows) from right to left and even-numbered rows

(usually WS rows) from left to right. Work the edge stitches, then work the stitches inside the repeat as many times as required. Some symbols may mean one thing on a RS row and another on a WS row (see above).

Once you have worked all the charted rows, start again at the bottom of the chart to begin the "row repeat" once more.

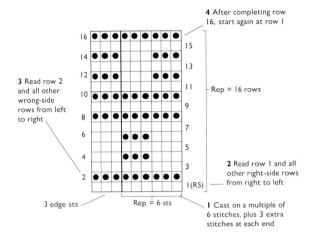

4 After completing row 16, start again at row 1

3 Read row 2 and all other wrong-side rows from left to right

Rep = 16 rows

2 Read row 1 and all other right-side rows from right to left

3 edge sts   Rep = 6 sts   **1** Cast on a multiple of 6 stitches, plus 3 extra stitches at each end

measuring tension

Always knit a tension swatch before you start your knitting project in order to make sure that you can achieve the stitch size (tension) recommended in your pattern. Only if you achieve the correct tension will your finished knitted fabric have the correct measurements for the garment or accessory.

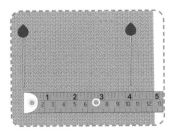

1 Using the specified needle size, knit a swatch about 13cm (5in) square. Mark 10cm (4in) across the centre of your swatch with pins and count the number of stitches between the pins.

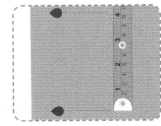

2 Count the number of rows to 10cm (4in) in the same way. If you have fewer stitches and rows than you should, try again with a smaller needle size; if you have more, change to a larger needle size.

Key techniques

Learning to knit is a very quick process. There are only a few key techniques you need to grasp before you are ready to make simple items like baby blankets. The basics include casting stitches onto and off the needle, knit and purl stitches, and knowing how to correct simple mistakes.

knit-on cast on (also called knit-stitch cast on)

The knit-on cast on is ideal for a beginner knitter because it uses the knit stitch as its foundation. Keep all of your stitches on the left needle and knit in to the last stitch. Keep your tension loose during the cast on or your stitches may turn out to be too tight and hard to work when forming the next stitch.

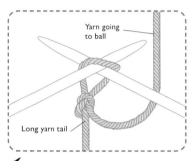

1 Make a slip knot and place it on one needle. Holding the yarn in the left or right hand, place the needle with the slip knot in the left hand. Insert the tip of the right needle from left to right through the centre of the loop on the left needle.

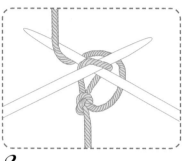

2 With the yarn behind the needles, wrap it under and around the tip of the right needle. (While casting on, use the left forefinger or middle finger to hold the loops on the left needle in position.)

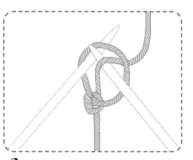

3 With the tip of the right needle, carefully draw the yarn through the loop on the left needle. (This is the same way a knit stitch is formed, hence the name of the cast on.)

4 Transfer the loop on the right needle to the left needle by inserting the tip of the left needle from right to left through the front of the loop.

5 Pull both yarn ends to tighten the new cast on loop on the needle, sliding it up close to the slip knot.

6 Continue casting on stitches in the same way until you have the required number of stitches. For a looser cast on, hold two needles together in your left hand whilst casting on.

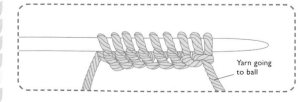

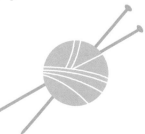

double cast on (also called long-tail cast on)

This cast on technique uses two strands of yarn, but only one needle; the resulting stitches are strong, elastic, and versatile. It is usually followed by a wrong side (WS) row, unless the reverse is the right side (RS). Start with a slip knot made after a long tail at least three times as long as the planned knitting width.

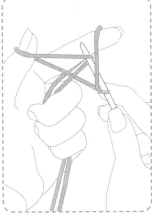

1 Make a slip knot on the needle, leaving a very long yarn tail – allow about 3.5cm (1⅜in) for each stitch being cast on. Hold the needle in your right hand. Then loop the yarn tail over the left thumb and the ball yarn end over the left forefinger as shown. Hold both strands in the palm of the left hand.

2 Insert the tip of the needle under and up through the loop on the thumb.

3 Wrap the tip of the needle around the loop on the forefinger from right to left and use it to pull the yarn through the loop on the thumb as shown by the arrow.

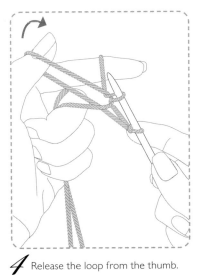

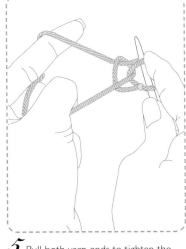

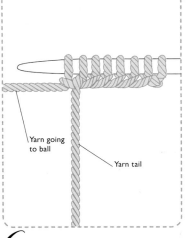

4 Release the loop from the thumb.

5 Pull both yarn ends to tighten the new cast on loop on the needle, sliding it up close to the slip knot.

6 Loop the yarn around the thumb again and cast on another stitch in the same way. Make as many stitches as you need.

casting off knitwise

When your piece of knitted fabric is complete you need to close off the loops so that they can't unravel. This is called casting off the stitches. Although casting off is shown below worked across knit stitches, the principle is the same for purl stitches. If instructed to retain stitches for future use, slip your stitches onto a spare needle or a stitch holder.

1 Begin by knitting the first two stitches. Then insert the tip of the left needle from left to right through the first stitch and lift this stitch up and over the second stitch and off the right needle.

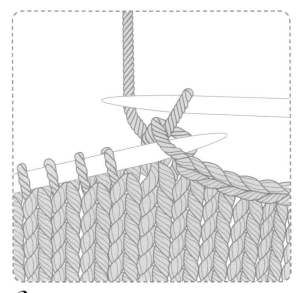

2 To cast off the next stitch, knit one more stitch and repeat step 1. Continue until only one stitch remains on the right needle. (If your pattern says "cast off in pattern", work the stitches in the specified pattern as you cast off.)

3 To stop the last stitch from unravelling, cut the yarn, leaving a yarn tail 20cm (8in) long, which is long enough to darn into the knitting later. (Alternatively, leave a much longer yarn end to use for a future seam.) Pass the yarn end through the remaining loop and pull tight to close the loop. This is called fastening off.

three-needle cast off

Try using this technique to add interest to your project. This can be worked on the right side of the knitting (as here) to form a decorative seam, or on the wrong side.

Consider using a contrast colour to complement your project. An adaptation of the three-needle cast off may even be used to smoothly integrate pockets and hems.

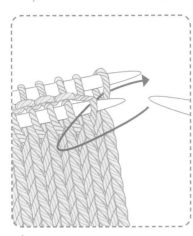  

1 Hold the needles with the stitches to be joined together with the wrong sides facing each other. Insert a third needle through the centre of the first stitch on each needle and knit these two stitches together.

2 Continue to knit together one stitch from each needle as you cast off the stitches in the usual way.

3 When the pieces of knitting are opened out, you will see that this technique forms a raised chain along the seam.

---

slipping stitches off needle

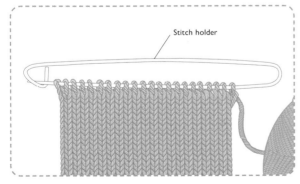

Stitch holder

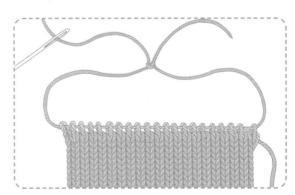

Using a stitch holder: If you are setting stitches aside to work on later, your instructions will tell you whether to cut the yarn or keep it attached to the ball. Carefully slip your stitches onto a stitch holder large enough to hold all the stitches. If you are only slipping a few stitches, use a safety pin.

Using a length of yarn: If you don't have a stitch holder or don't have one large enough, you can use a length of cotton yarn instead. Using a blunt-ended yarn needle, pass the yarn through the stitches as you slip them off the knitting needle. Knot the ends of the cotton yarn together.

knit stitch (k)

All knitting is made up of two basic stitches – knit and purl. Garter stitch (see p.215) uses only knit stitch. Try out fun stripes and different yarns in garter stitch to perfect your knit stitch. The odd dropped stitch does not matter while you're experimenting, put a safety pin through it so it does not drop further and sew it in later.

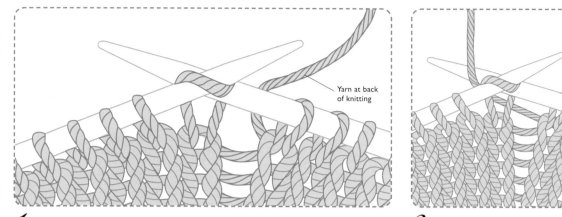

Yarn at back of knitting

1 Hold the needle with the unworked stitches in your left hand and the other needle in your right hand. With the yarn at the back of the knitting, insert the tip of the right needle from left to right under the front loop and through the centre of the next stitch to be worked on the left needle.

2 Wrap the yarn under and around the tip of the right needle, keeping an even tension as the yarn slips through your fingers.

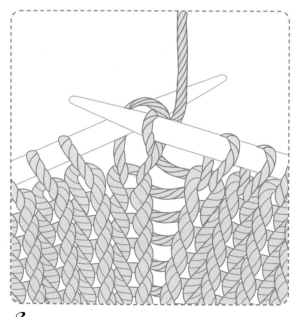

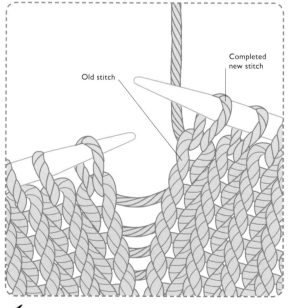

Old stitch

Completed new stitch

3 With the tip of the right needle, carefully draw the yarn through the stitch on the left needle. Hold the yarn firmly but not too tightly.

4 Let the old loop drop off the left needle to complete the knit stitch on the right needle.

purl stitch (p)

Purl stitch is a little more difficult than knit stitch, but like knit stitch it becomes effortless with practice. Once you are a seasoned knitter, you will feel as if you could work these basic stitches in your sleep. You may find your tension alters on purl stitches, so try holding your yarn a little tighter or looser to compensate.

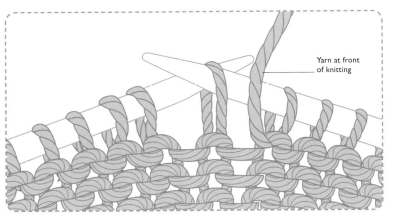

Yarn at front of knitting

1 Hold the needle with the unworked stitches in your left hand and the other needle in your right hand. With the yarn at the front of the knitting, insert the tip of the right needle from right to left through the centre of the next stitch to be worked on the left needle.

2 Wrap the yarn over and around the tip of the right needle. Keep an even tension on the yarn as you release it through your fingers.

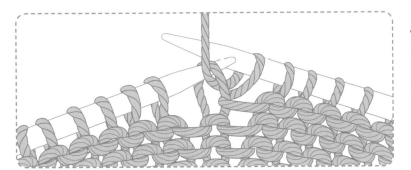

3 With the tip of the right needle, carefully draw the yarn through the stitch on the left needle. Keep your hands relaxed and allow the yarn to slip through your fingers in a gently controlled manner.

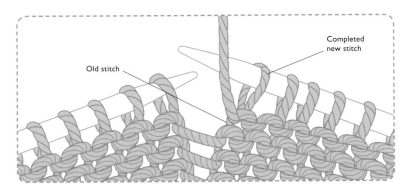

Completed new stitch

Old stitch

4 Let the old loop drop off the left needle to complete the purl stitch.

The edge of the
Flower bobble
beanie rolls up
naturally.
(See pp.162–165)

basic knit and purl stitches

Once you know how to work knit and purl stitches with ease, you will be able to work the most frequently used stitch patterns – garter stitch, stocking stitch, and single ribbing. Stocking stitch is commonly used for plain knitted items, as in the Flower bobble beanie, left, and garter stitch and single ribbing for garment edging.

Garter stitch (g st)

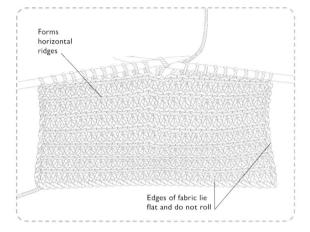

Forms horizontal ridges

Edges of fabric lie flat and do not roll

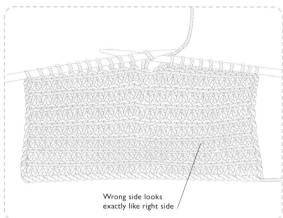

Wrong side looks exactly like right side

Knit right-side (RS) rows: Garter stitch is the easiest of all knitted fabrics as all rows are worked in knit stitches. When the right side of the fabric is facing you, knit all the stitches in the row.

Knit wrong-side (WS) rows: When the wrong side of the fabric is facing you, knit all the stitches in the row. The resulting fabric is soft, textured, and slightly stretchy.

Stocking stitch (st st)

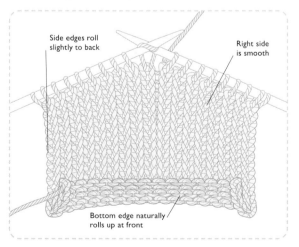

Side edges roll slightly to back

Right side is smooth

Bottom edge naturally rolls up at front

Wrong side is knobbly

Knit right-side (RS) rows: Stocking stitch is formed by working alternate rows of knit and purl stitches. When the right side is facing you, knit all the stitches in the row.

Purl wrong-side (WS) rows: When the wrong side is facing you, purl all the stitches in the row. The wrong side is often referred to as the "purl side" of the knitting.

Single ribbing (k1, p1 rib)

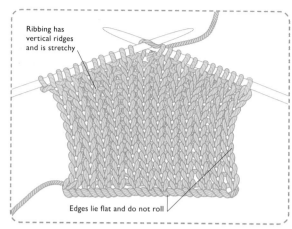

Ribbing has vertical ridges and is stretchy

Edges lie flat and do not roll

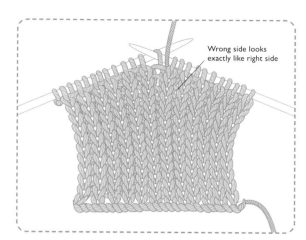

Wrong side looks exactly like right side

Right-side (RS) rows: Single ribbing is formed by working alternate knit and purl stitches. After a knit stitch, take the yarn to the front of the knitting to purl the next stitch. After a purl stitch, take the yarn to the back to knit the next stitch.

Wrong-side (WS) rows: On the wrong-side rows, knit all the knit stitches that are facing you and purl all the purl stitches. Work the following rows in the same way to form thin columns of alternating single knit and purl stitches.

correcting mistakes

These useful techniques will help you to complete your work if you run into any problems. The best thing to do if you make a mistake in your knitting is to unravel it back to the mistake by unpicking the stitches one by one. If you drop a stitch, be sure to pick it up quickly before it comes undone right back to the cast on edge.

Unpicking a knit row

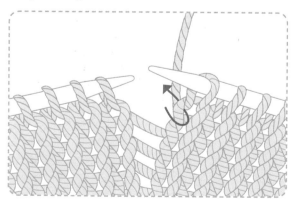

Hold the needle with the stitches in your right hand. To unpick each stitch individually, insert the tip of the left needle from front to back through the stitch below the first knit stitch on the right needle, then drop the old knit stitch off the needle and pull out the loop.

Unpicking a purl row

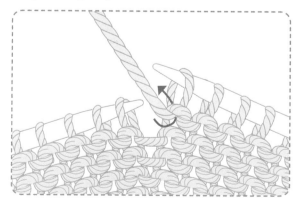

Hold the needle with the stitches in your right hand. Unpick each purl stitch individually with the tip of the left needle in the same way as for the knit stitch.

Picking up a dropped stitch

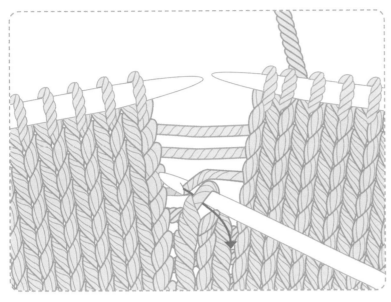

If you drop a stitch on stocking stitch, you can easily reclaim it with a crochet hook. With the right side of the knitting facing you, insert the hook through the dropped loop. Catch the strand between the stitches and pull a loop through the loop on the hook. Continue up the rows in this way until you reach the top. Then slip the stitch back onto your needle.

Picking up and working a missed yarnover in lace knitting and increasing

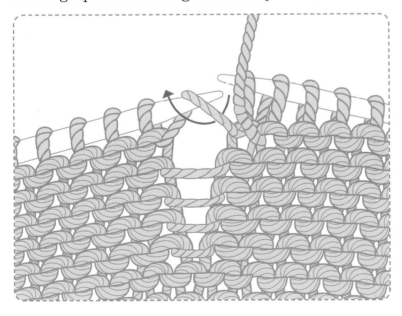

Count your stitches often when knitting lace to make sure you have the right number of stitches. If you are missing a stitch you may have left out a yarnover. There is no need to undo stitches all the way back to the mistake. Simply work to the position of the missing yarnover on the following row, then insert the left needle from front to back under the strand between the stitch just worked and the next stitch on the left needle (see left). Work this stitch through the front of the loop in the usual way, shown as purl in this example.

Understanding written instructions

Some stitch patterns will call for "slipping" stitches and knitting "through the back of the loop". These useful techniques are given next as a handy reference when you are consulting the abbreviations list on page 206.

Slipping stitches purlwise

1 Always slip stitches purlwise, for example when slipping stitches onto a stitch holder, unless instructed otherwise. Insert the tip of the right needle from right to left through the front of the loop on the left needle.

2 Slide the stitch onto the right needle and off the left needle without working it. The slipped stitch now sits on the right needle with the right side of the loop at the front just like the worked stitches next to it.

Slipping stitches knitwise

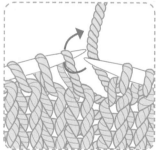

1 Slip stitches knitwise only if instructed to do so or if working decreases (see pp.224–227), as it twists the stitch. First insert the tip of the right needle from left to right through the front of the loop on the left needle.

2 Slide the stitch onto the right needle and off the left needle without working it. The slipped stitch now sits on the right needle with the left side of the loop at the front of the needle unlike the worked stitches next to it.

Knitting through back of loop (k1 tbl)

1 When row instructions say "k1 tbl" (knit one through the back of the loop), insert the right needle from right to left through the side of the stitch behind the left needle (called the back of the loop).

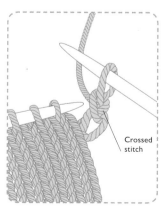

2 Wrap the yarn around the tip of the right needle and complete the knit stitch in the usual way. This twists the stitch in the row below so that the legs of the stitch cross at the base. (The same principle applies for working p1 tbl, k2tog tbl, and p2tog tbl.)

Crossed stitch

Increases and decreases

Increasing or decreasing the number of stitches on the needle is the way knitting is shaped, changing the edges from straight to curves and slants. Increases and decreases are also used in combinations with knit and purl stitches to form interesting textures and effects, including lace.

simple increases

The following techniques are simple increases used for shaping knitting. They create one extra stitch without creating a visible hole and are called invisible increases.

Multiple increases, which add more than one extra stitch, are used less frequently and are always explained fully in the knitting pattern.

Knit into front and back of stitch (kfb or inc 1)

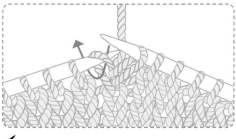

1 Knit the next stitch, leaving the stitch being worked on the left needle. Insert the right needle through the back of the loop from right to left. This popular invisible increase for a knit row is also called a bar increase because it creates a little bar between the stitches.

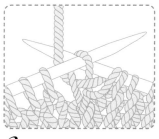

2 Wrap the yarn around the tip of the right needle, draw the yarn through the loop to form the second stitch and drop the old stitch off the left needle.

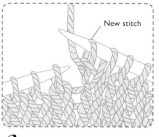

New stitch

3 Knitting into the front and the back of the stitch creates two stitches out of one and increases one stitch in the row.

Purl into front and back of stitch (pfb or inc 1)

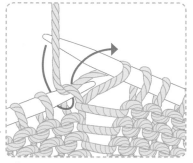

1 Purl the next stitch, leaving the stitch being worked on the left needle. Insert the right needle through the back of the loop from left to right.

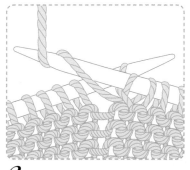

2 Wrap the yarn around the tip of the right needle, draw the yarn through the loop to form the second stitch and drop the old stitch off the left needle.

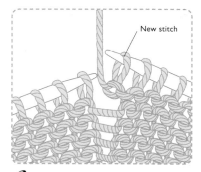

New stitch

3 Purling into the front and the back of the stitch like this creates two stitches out of one and increases one stitch in the row.

Lifted increase on knit row (inc 1)

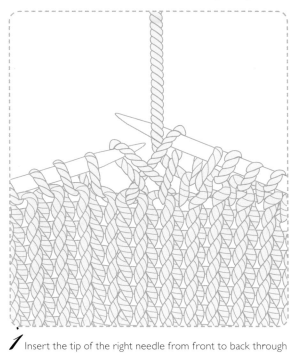

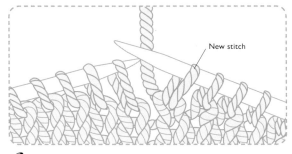

2 Knit the next stitch (the stitch above the lifted stitch on the left needle) in the usual way.

1 Insert the tip of the right needle from front to back through the stitch below the next stitch on the left needle. Knit this lifted loop.

3 This creates two stitches out of one and increases one stitch in the row. (The purl version of this stitch is worked using the same principle.)

"Make-one" increase on a knit row (M1 or M1k)

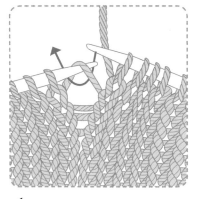

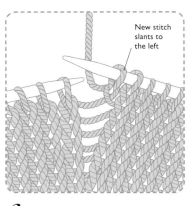

1 Insert the tip of the left needle from front to back under the horizontal strand between the stitch just knit and the next stitch. Then insert the right needle through the strand on the left needle from right to left behind the left needle.

2 Wrap the yarn around the tip of the right needle and draw the yarn through the lifted loop. (This is called knitting through the back of the loop.)

3 This creates an extra stitch in the row. (Knitting through the back of the loop twists the base of the new stitch to produce a crossed stitch that closes up the hole it would have created.)

"Make-one" increase on a purl row (MI or MIp)

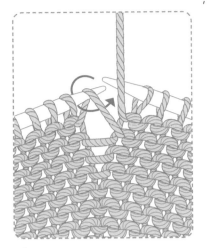 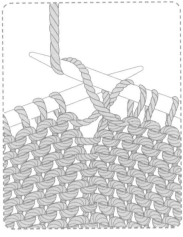

1 Insert the tip of the left needle from front to back under the horizontal strand between the stitch just knit and the next stitch. Then insert the right needle through the strand on the left needle from left to right behind the left needle.

2 Wrap the yarn around the tip of the right needle and draw the yarn through the lifted loop (known as purling through the back of the loop).

3 This creates an extra stitch in the row. (Purling through the back of the loop twists the base of the new stitch to produce a crossed stitch that closes up the hole it would have created.)

Multiple increases ([kl, pl, kl] into next st)

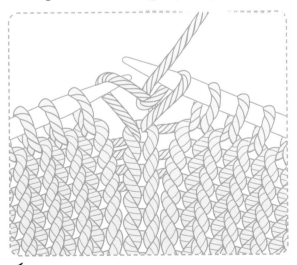 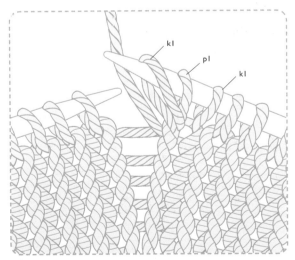

1 To begin the increase, knit the next stitch but leave the old stitch on the left needle. This is a very easy increase if you need to add more than one stitch to an existing stitch, but it does create a small hole under the new stitches.

2 Then purl and knit into the same loop on the left needle. This action is called knit one, purl one, knit one all into the next stitch. It creates two extra stitches in the row. You can keep alternating k and p stitches in the same loop to create more stitches if desired.

yarnover increases

Yarnover increases add stitches to a row and create holes, so are often called visible increases. A yarnover is made by looping the yarn around the right needle to form an extra stitch. Wrap the loop around the needle in the correct way or it will become crossed when it is worked in the next row, which closes the hole.

Yarnover between knit stitches (UK yfwd; US yo)

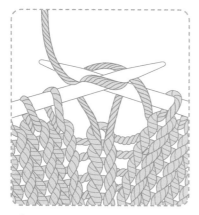

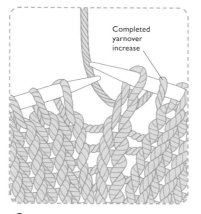

Completed yarnover increase

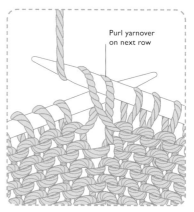

Purl yarnover on next row

1 Bring the yarn forward (yfwd) to the front of the knitting between the needles. Take the yarn over the top of the right needle to the back and work the next knit stitch in the usual way.

2 When the knit stitch is complete, the yarnover is correctly formed on the right needle with the right leg of the loop at the front.

3 On the following row, when you reach the yarnover, purl it through the front of the loop in the usual way. This creates an open hole under the purl stitch.

Yarnover between purl stitches (UK yrn; US yo)

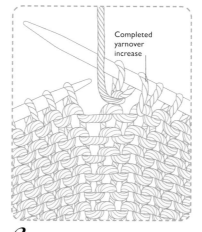

Completed yarnover increase

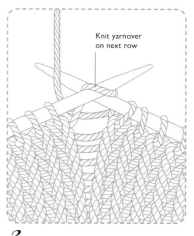

Knit yarnover on next row

1 Bring the yarn to the back of the work over the top of the right needle, then to the front between the needles. Work the next purl stitch in the usual way.

2 When the purl stitch is complete, the yarnover is correctly formed on the right needle with the right leg of the loop at the front of the needle.

3 On the following row, when you reach the yarnover, knit it through the front of the loop in the usual way. This creates an open hole under the knit stitch.

Yarnover between knit and purl stitches (UK yfrn and yon; US yo)

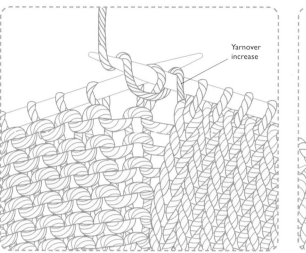

Yarnover increase

Yarnover increase

After a knit stitch and before a purl stitch (yfrn): Bring the yarn to the front between the needles, then over the top of the right needle and to the front again. Purl the next stitch. On the following row, work the yarnover through the front of the loop in the usual way to create an open hole.

After a purl stitch and before a knit stitch (yon): Take the yarn over the top of the right needle and to the back of the work, then knit the next stitch. On the following row, work the yarnover through the front of the loop in the usual way to create an open hole.

Yarnover at the beginning of a row (UK yfwd and yrn; US yo)

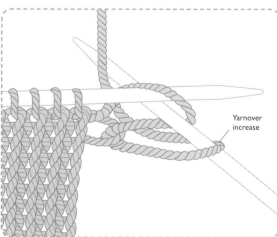

Yarnover increase

Yarnover increase

At the beginning of a row before a knit stitch (yfwd): Insert the tip of the right needle behind the yarn and into the first stitch knitwise. Then take the yarn over the top of the right needle to the back and complete the knit stitch. On the following row, work the yarnover through the front of the loop in the usual way to create an open scallop at the edge.

At the beginning of a row before a purl stitch (yrn): Wrap the yarn from front to back over the top of the right needle and to the front again between the needles. Then purl the first stitch. On the following row, work the yarnover through the front of the loop in the usual way to create an open scallop at the edge.

Closed yarnover on garter stitch

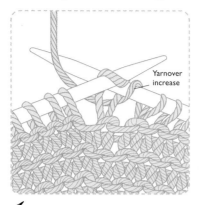

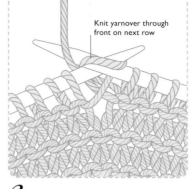
Yarnover increase

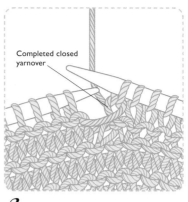
Knit yarnover through front on next row

Completed closed yarnover

1 This is used as an "invisible" increase and is especially good for garter stitch. Take the yarn from back to front over the top of the right needle, then around the needle to the back of the work between the needles. Knit the next stitch in the usual way.

2 On the next row, knit the yarnover through the front loop (the strand at the front of the left needle).

3 This creates a crossed stitch and closes the yarnover hole. Although the crossed stitch is similar to the one made with a make-one increase (see pp.220–221), it is looser, which is perfect for the loose garter stitch texture.

simple decreases

These simple decreases are often used for shaping knitting and, paired with increases, for textured stitches. More complicated decreases are always explained in knitting instructions. Most of the decreases that follow are single decreases that subtract only one stitch from the knitting, but a few double decreases are included.

Knit two together (k2tog or dec 1)

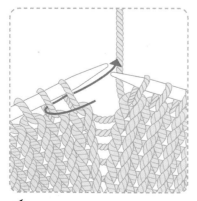

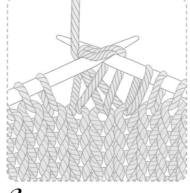

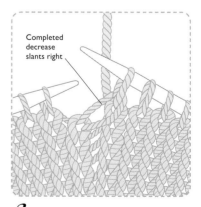
Completed decrease slants right

1 Insert the tip of the right needle from left to right through the second stitch and the first stitch on the left needle.

2 Wrap the yarn around the tip of the right needle, draw the yarn through both loops and drop the old stitches off the left needle.

3 This makes two stitches into one and decreases one stitch in the row. The completed stitch slants to the right.

Purl two together (p2tog or dec 1)

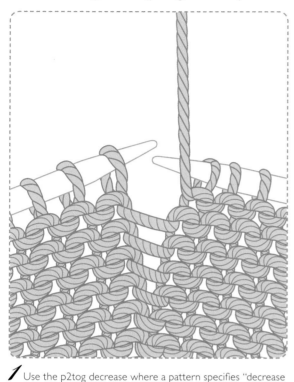

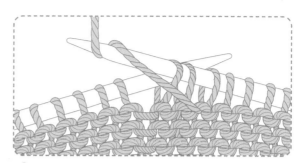

2 Wrap the yarn around the tip of the right needle, draw the yarn through both loops and drop the old stitches off the left needle.

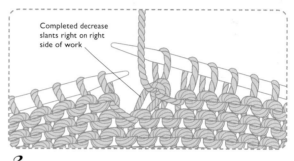

Completed decrease slants right on right side of work

1 Use the p2tog decrease where a pattern specifies "decrease 1" on a purl row. Insert the tip of the right needle from right to left through the first then the second stitch on the left needle.

3 This makes two stitches into one and decreases one stitch in the row.

Slip one, knit one, pass slipped stitch over (sl k1 psso or skpo)

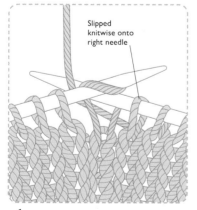

Slipped knitwise onto right needle

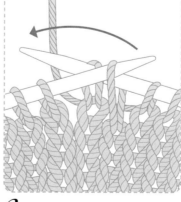

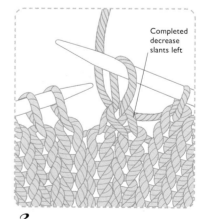

Completed decrease slants left

1 Slip the first stitch on the left needle knitwise (see p.218) onto the right needle without working it. Knit the next stitch.

2 Pick up the slipped stitch with the tip of the left needle and pass it over the knit stitch and off the right needle.

3 This makes two stitches into one and decreases one stitch in the row.

Slip, slip, knit (ssk)

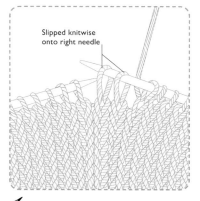

Slipped knitwise onto right needle

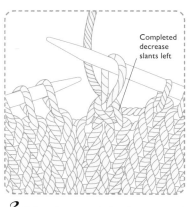

Completed decrease slants left

1 Slip the next two stitches on the left needle knitwise (see p.218), one at a time, onto the right needle without working them.

2 Insert the tip of the left needle from left to right through the fronts of the two slipped stitches (the right needle is now behind the left). Knit these two stitches together.

3 This makes two stitches into one and decreases one stitch in the row.

Slip, slip, purl (ssp)

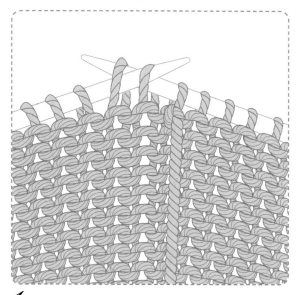

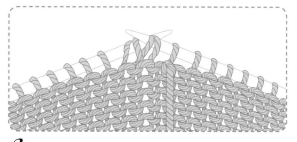

3 Holding the right needle at the back, bring the tip upwards from left to right through the back of the two stitches, bringing the right needle in front of the left as it comes through the stitches.

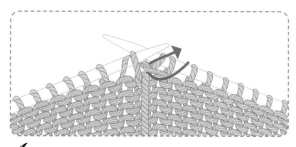

1 Keeping yarn at the front, slip two stitches, one at a time, knitwise (see p.218) onto the right needle without working them as for ssk decrease above.

2 Holding the needles tip to tip, insert the left needle into both stitches and transfer back to the left needle without twisting them.

4 Lay the yarn between the needles as for purl. Take the right needle down and back through both loops, then slide them off the left needle together. This makes one stitch out of the two, and decreases one stitch in the row.

Double decreases

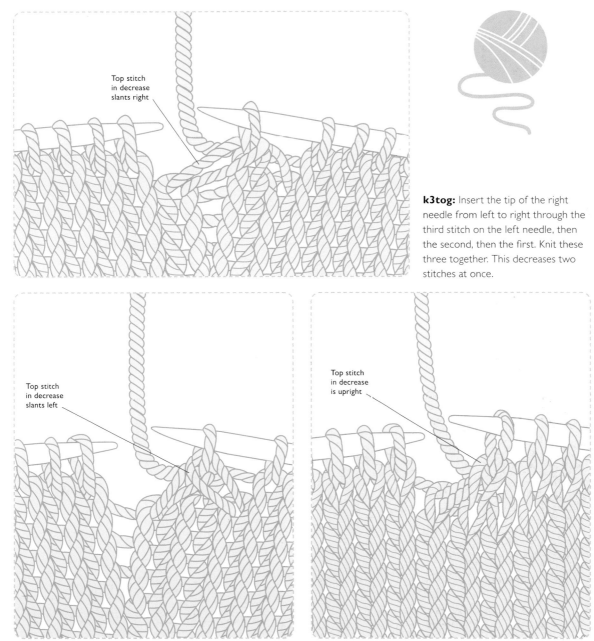

Top stitch
in decrease
slants right

k3tog: Insert the tip of the right needle from left to right through the third stitch on the left needle, then the second, then the first. Knit these three together. This decreases two stitches at once.

Top stitch
in decrease
slants left

Top stitch
in decrease
is upright

s1 k2tog psso (sk2p): Slip one stitch knitwise onto the right needle, knit the next two stitches together, then pass the slipped stitch over the k2tog and off the right needle. This decreases two stitches at once.

s2 k1 p2sso: Slip two stitches knitwise together onto the right needle, knit the next stitch, then pass the two slipped stitches together over the knit stitch and off the right needle. This decreases two stitches at once.

Twists

If you are looking for textures with higher relief and more sculptural qualities, twists are a useful technique to learn. Twists are made by crossing stitches over each other in different ways to form an array of intricate patterns.

simple twists

A simple twist is made over two stitches, without a cable needle. Although twists do not create such high relief as cables, their subtlety make them popular. The following twists are worked in stocking stitch on a stocking stitch ground. They can also be worked with one knit and one purl stitch – the principle is the same.

Right twist (T2R)

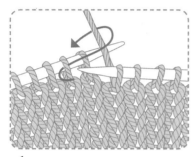 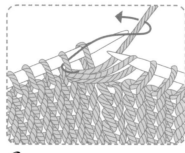 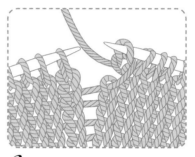

1 With yarn at the back of the right needle and in front of the left, knit the second stitch leaving the first and second stitches on the left needle.

2 Knit the first stitch on the left needle and drop both old stitches off the left needle at the same time.

3 Without the use of a cable needle, this creates a "one-over-one" two-stitch cable slanting to the right – called a right twist.

Left twist (T2L)

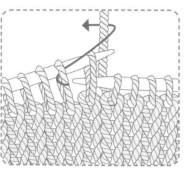 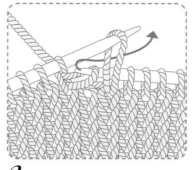 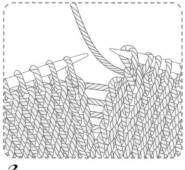

1 Insert the tip of the right needle behind the first stitch on the left needle and through the second stitch knitwise. Wrap the yarn around the right needle.

2 Pull the loop through the second stitch behind the first stitch. Be careful not to drop either the first or second stitches off the left needle yet.

3 Knit the first stitch on the left needle and drop both old stitches off the left needle. This creates a two-stitch cable slanting to the left – called a left twist.

I-cord

I-cord stands for "idiot" cord and is also known as slip cord. It is knitted on double-pointed needles and makes a neat edging or can be used for straps and ties, or for appliqué in a contrasting colour. When used for an edging it is best worked on smaller needles.

simple i-cord

These cords can be applied to an item later, so it is possible to add extra detail as they are worked. Stripes, texture, structural effects, and even beads can be incorporated. With its simple method but multiple uses, i-cord is a very versatile technique that you will use over and over again.

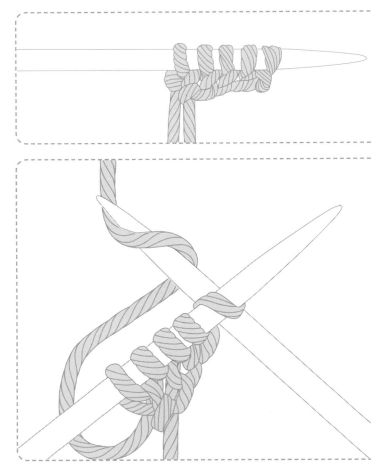

1 Cast on five stitches using a single cast on. Knit one row. Transfer the needle to your left hand without turning it and slide all the stitches to the right end of the needle, so that the yarn appears to be at the wrong end to knit another row.

2 Insert the right needle into the first stitch on the left needle, pull the yarn firmly from the left side of the knitting around the back to knit the first stitch. Tug the yarn again to pull the knitting round into a tube.

3 Repeat steps 1 and 2, starting from when you transfer the needle, until the cord is the required length.

Short rows

Short rowing, or "partial knitting", involves knitting two rows across some of the stitches, thereby adding rows in only one part of the fabric. It is popular for creating smooth edges in shoulder shaping, curving hems, and turning sock heels.

preventing holes

In most shaping applications a concealed turn is required and there are two ways in which to work this: the "wrap" or "tie" and the "catch" are shown here.

Garter stitch, which uses only knit stitches on both RS and WS rows, does not require any wrapping.

Wrap or tie to close holes

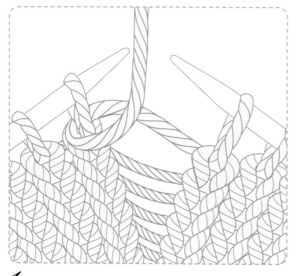

1 On a knit row: at turn position, slip next stitch purlwise onto right needle (see p.218), yarn to front. Return slip stitch to left needle, yarn back. Turn and purl short row. Repeat wrap at each mid-row turn.

2 On a purl row: at turn, slip next stitch purlwise, yarn to back. Slip stitch back, yarn to front. Turn and knit short row. Repeat wrap at each mid-row turn.

3 When working across all stitches on completion of short rowing: at wrap, insert right needle up through front (knit) or back (purl) of wrap. Work wrap together with next stitch.

Catch to close holes

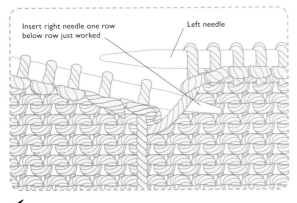

Insert right needle one row below row just worked

Left needle

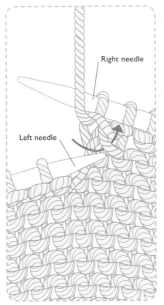

Right needle

Left needle

1 On either knit or purl rows, work a short row. Turn work, slip first stitch purlwise (see p.218), and work back along short row.

2 When knitting a completion row (knitting is shown temporarily reversed as this makes this step easier), insert right needle down through strand between first and second stitches on left needle as shown. Lift onto left needle.

3 Turn work again and knit picked up loop together with next stitch on left needle.

4 If completion row is purl, insert left needle upwards through the strand between the first and second stitch two rows below right needle. Stretch this loop, then drop it. Slip next stitch from left to right needle. Pick up dropped loop again with the left needle. Return slipped stitch to left needle. Purl these two together.

smooth diagonal cast off

This cast off is particularly suitable for neat shoulder seams on baby garments. This example assumes you are working a pattern with a diagonal edge to cast off in groups of five.

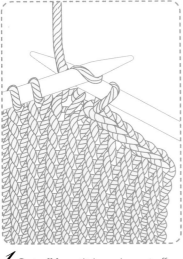

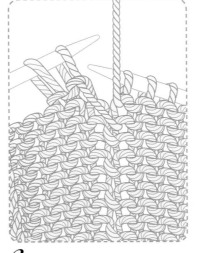

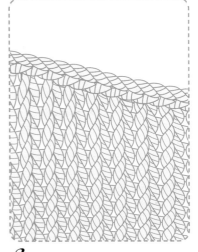

1 Cast off four stitches using cast off knitwise method, leaving the last stitch of the cast off on the right needle.

2 Knit to the end of the row on the left needle, turn the work and purl until there are only two stitches remaining on the left needle.

3 Purl these two stitches together. Turn the work. Repeat until the cast off length is completed.

Shaping: adapting a cast off shoulder to short row shaping

1 This shows adapting a stocking stitch pattern with cast off shoulder shaping. If the instruction is to cast off 8 stitches every alternate row, then 8 less stitches must be knitted every alternate row. The outer edge of a shoulder is lower than the neck edge, so short rows must be built up at the end of knit rows.

2 To practise this technique, work with a multiple of 8 stitches (24 stitches shown). Work the row with the first shoulder cast off instruction, but do not cast off any stitches. Turn work.

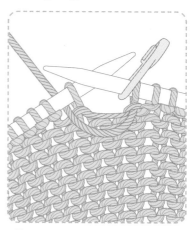

3 Purl to 8 stitches from the end and work a wrap (slip next stitch purlwise, yarn back, return slip stitch, yarn forwards). Turn and knit to end.

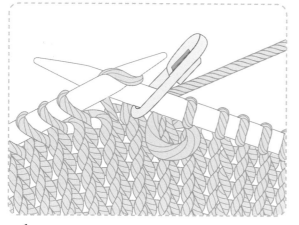

4 Turn work. Purl to 16 stitches from the end of the row, work wrap, and turn. Knit to the end (8 stitches on needle).

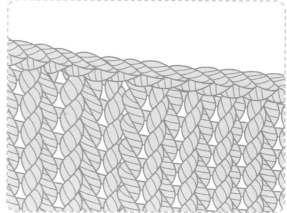

5 Turn work. Purl across all the stitches, picking up wraps by slipping them onto left needle and purling together with next stitch. Either cast off all stitches, or put them onto a stitch holder for grafting later. This gives you a smooth diagonal shoulder line. Grafting together two short row shaped shoulders makes an ideal seam for babywear.

Colourwork

If you like adding colours to your knitting there are a number of methods to use. The easiest is to knit using a multicoloured yarn, which changes colour along the strand. To add colours into the knitting yourself, you can work simple stripes, charted intarsia motifs, or Fair Isle.

simple stripes

Horizontal stripes are perfect for knitters who want to have fun with colour without learning more advanced techniques. There are an infinite variety of stripe widths, colours, and textures possible. You can follow any plainly coloured pattern and introduce stripes without affecting the tension or shape of the knitting.

Two-colour garter stitch stripe

This stripe pattern is worked in garter stitch in two colours (A and B). To work the stripe, knit two rows in each colour alternately, dropping the colour not in use at the side of the work and picking it up when it is needed again.

Tidying the edges

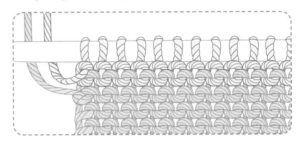

When working two coloured, even row stripes, twist the yarns around each other every 1–2cm (½–¾in) up the side of the piece. Alternating the direction of the twist after each colour change prevents the yarns becoming tangled.

charted colourwork

The technique for charted stocking stitch colourwork opens up a world of designs. In intarsia, a separate length of yarn is used for each colour and the yarns are twisted together at the colour-change junctures. In Fair Isle, a yarn colour is stranded across the wrong side of the work until it is required.

Following a colourwork chart

The first step in understanding charted colourwork is to grasp how easy the charts are to follow. Rather than writing it out, your knitting pattern provides a chart with colours marked in symbols or in blocks of colour.

If a pattern covers the whole garment, a large chart is provided for each element with all the stitches for the entire piece. Where a pattern is a repeat, the repeat alone is charted. Each square on a stocking stitch colourwork chart represents a stitch and each horizontal row of squares represents a knitted row. Follow the chart from bottom to top.

The key provided with the chart tells you which colour to use for each stitch. All odd-numbered rows are usually right side (knit) rows and are read from right to left. All even-numbered rows are usually wrong side (purl) rows and are read from left to right. Always read your knitting pattern instructions carefully to make sure that the chart follows these general rules.

The Dino jumper is a fun intarsia project to try out.
(See pp.20–23)

intarsia chart

This heart is an example of a simple intarsia colourwork chart. Each colour on the chart is represented by a different symbol. The blank squares around the motif (the background) also represent a colour.
You can tell that a charted design should be worked in the intarsia technique if a colour appears only in a section of a row and is not needed across the entire row. Use a separate long length of yarn, or yarn on a bobbin, for each area of colour in intarsia knitting (including separated background areas). Twist the colours where they meet (see below).

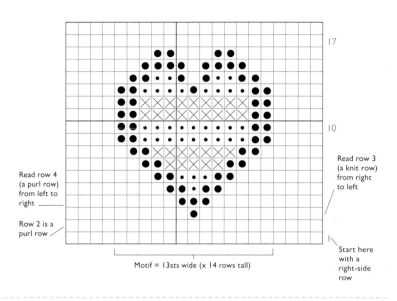

17

10

Read row 3
(a knit row)
from right
to left

Read row 4
(a purl row)
from left to
right

Row 2 is a
purl row

Start here
with a
right-side
row

Motif = 13sts wide (x 14 rows tall)

KEY

□ = background colour   ◉ = motif colour 1
● = motif colour 2   ⊠ = motif colour 3

intarsia technique

In the intarsia technique each yarn is worked separately. Each colour in a row must have its own small ball of yarn. Cut short lengths from the main balls and wind onto bobbins to prevent tangles.

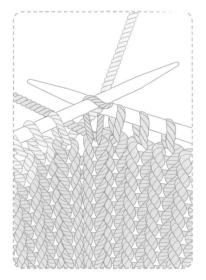

Right-slant colour change: To avoid holes, twist the colours around each other only on the knit rows.

Left-slant colour change: To avoid holes, twist the colours around each other only on the purl rows.

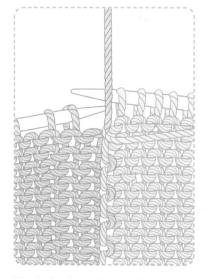

Vertical colour change: To avoid holes, twist the colours around each other on both knit and purl rows.

Circular knitting

Circular knitting, or knitting in the round, is worked on a circular needle or with a set of four or five double-pointed needles. With the right side always facing outwards, the knitting is worked round and round to form a tube.

knitting tubes

For those who don't enjoy stitching seams, knitting seamless tubes is a real bonus. Large tubes can be worked on a long circular needle. Short circular needles are used for seamless neckbands and armhole bands, and hats. Double-pointed needles are used for smaller items, such as mittens and socks.

Working with a circular knitting needle

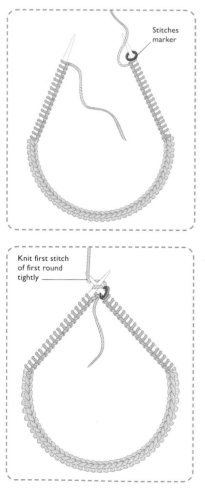

Stitches marker

Knit first stitch of first round tightly

1 Cast on the required number of stitches. Ensure that the stitches are untwisted and they all face inwards, then slip a stitch marker onto the end of the right needle to mark the beginning of the round.

2 Hold the needle ends in your hands and bring the right needle up to the left needle to work the first stitch. Knit round and round on the stitches. When the stitch marker is reached, slip it from the left needle to the right needle.

3 If you are working a stocking stitch tube on a circular needle, the right side of the work will always be facing you and every round will be a knit round.

Joining the circle of stitches

This is a neat way of closing the circle in circular knitting.

1 Cast on required number of stitches, plus one stitch.

2 Slip the first cast on stitch onto the right needle, next to last cast on stitch. Place the join marker after this stitch.

3 Knit the round, then at the end, knit the last two stitches before the marker together (this is the first cast on stitch and the extra stitch).

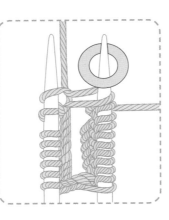

Working with a set of four double-pointed needles

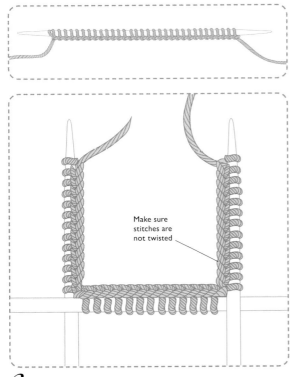

Make sure stitches are not twisted

1 Your knitting instructions will specify how many double-pointed needles to use for the project you are making – either a set of four or a set of five. When working with a set of four double-pointed needles, first cast on all the stitches required onto a single needle.

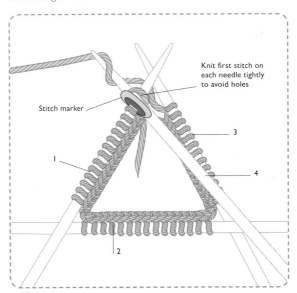

Knit first stitch on each needle tightly to avoid holes

Stitch marker

1

2

3

4

2 Slip some of the stitches off onto two other needles – your knitting pattern will tell you precisely how many to place on each needle. Ensure that the bottoms of the cast on loops are all facing inwards.

3 Place a stitch marker between the first and second stitches on the first needle to mark the beginning of the round. Then pull the first and third needles close together and start to knit with the fourth needle. Knit round and round in this way as for knitting with a circular needle (see opposite).

Finishing details

Finishing, as its name suggests, is the final stage of a project. Details that will make your knitting easier to assemble and look more professional, such as adding borders, hems, pockets, and fastenings, can, with a little planning, be incorporated into the actual knitting itself.

picking up stitches

Picking up edging stitches is a technique that even experienced knitters can sometimes find challenging. Careful preparation and lots of practise will help, though. It's worth trying it out on small pieces of knitting to perfect the technique before moving on to more important projects.

Cast on/off edge

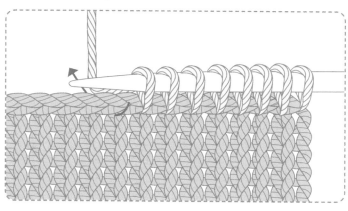

With RS facing, insert the needle in the first stitch. Leaving a long, loose yarn tail, wrap the yarn around the tip and pull it through, as if knitting a stitch. Continue, picking up and knitting one stitch through every cast on or cast off stitch.

Along row-ends

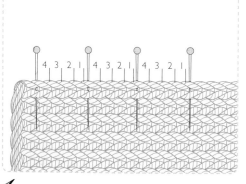

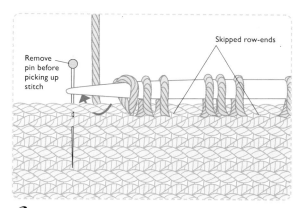

1 On light-weight or medium-weight yarn, pick up three stitches for every four row-ends. Mark out the row-ends on the right side of the knitting, placing a pin on the first of every four row-ends.

2 Pick up and knit the stitches as for picking up stitches along a cast on edge, inserting the tip through the centre of the edge stitches. Skip every fourth row-end.

With a crochet hook

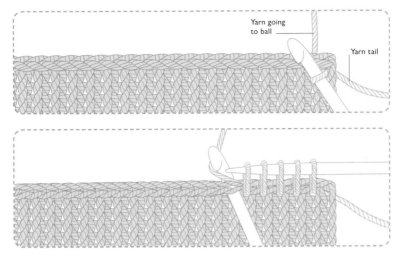

Yarn going to ball

Yarn tail

1 Use a hook that fits through the stitches. With RS facing, insert the hook through the first stitch, wrap the hook behind and around the yarn from left to right and pull through.

2 Transfer the loop on the hook onto a needle. Pull yarn to tighten. Repeat, transferring the loops to the needle.

Along a curved edge

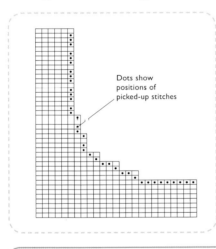

Dots show positions of picked-up stitches

1 When picking up stitches along a curved edge, pick up one stitch in each cast off stitch and three stitches for every four row-ends. Ignore the corner stitches along the stepped decreases to smooth out the curve.

2 Once all of the stitches have been picked up, work the border design as instructed in your knitting pattern.

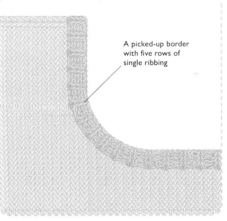

A picked-up border with five rows of single ribbing

🍃 Tips for picking up stitches

When picking up stitches use a matching yarn to hide picked-up imperfections. For a contrasting border, switch to the new colour on the first row of the border.

Always pick up and knit stitches with the right side of the knitting facing you, as picking up stitches creates a ridge on the wrong side.

Your knitting pattern will specify which needle size to use for picking up stitches – usually one size smaller than the size used for the main knitting.

After you have picked up the required number of stitches, work the border following the directions in your pattern, whether it is ribbing, moss stitch, garter stitch, or a fold-over hem.

If it is difficult to pick up stitches "evenly" along an edge, try casting it off again, either looser or tighter. If this doesn't work, pull out the border and try again, adjusting the number of stitches or spreading them out in a different way. Alternatively, try a smaller needle size if the border looks too stretched, or a larger needle size if it looks too tight.

blocking a finished item

Always refer to your yarn label before blocking. Textured stitch patterns, such as garter stitch and ribbing, are best wet blocked or steamed extremely gently so that their texture is not altered – they should not be pressed or stretched.

Wet blocking

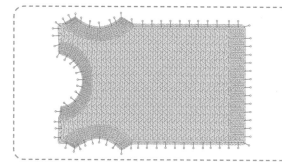

Wet blocking is best if your yarn allows. Use lukewarm water and either wash or wet the knitting. Squeeze it and lay it on a towel before rolling it up to remove more moisture. Pin into shape on another towel covered with a sheet. Leave to dry.

Steam blocking

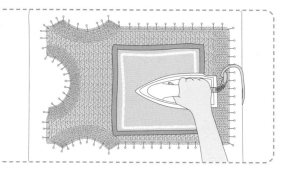

To steam block, pin the knitting to the correct shape, then place a damp cloth on top. Use a warm iron to create steam, but do not rest the iron on the knitting, and avoid any garter stitch or ribbed areas. Leave to dry completely before removing the pins.

sewing up seams

The most popular seam techniques for knitting are mattress stitch, edge-to-edge stitch, and backstitch. Cast off and grafted seams are sometimes called for and learning to graft open stitches together for a seamless join is very useful. Always secure the seaming yarn before you start.

Tips

Block knitted pieces before sewing together. After seams are completed, open them out and steam very lightly if the yarn allows.

Always use a blunt-ended yarn needle for all seams on knitting. A pointed needle will puncture the yarn strands and you won't be able to pull the yarn through the knitting successfully.

If knitting is in a fancy yarn, find a smooth strong yarn of a similar colour to sew up with. It is better with mattress stitch to work with shorter lengths as long strands may break.

Before starting a seam, pin the knitting together at wide intervals. Secure the yarn to the edge of one piece of knitting with two or three overcast stitches.

Make seams firm but not too tight. They should have a little elasticity, to match the elasticity of the knitted fabric.

Mattress stitch

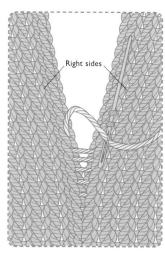

Right sides

1 Mattress stitch is almost invisible and is the best seam for ribbing and stocking stitch. Align the edges of the pieces with RS facing you.

2 Insert needle from the front through centre of first stitch on one piece and up through centre of stitch in row above. Repeat on the other piece, gently pulling seam closed every few stitches.

Join the seams
according to
the instructions
in your pattern.
(For Ballet wrap cardigan,
see pp.14–17)

Edge-to-edge seam

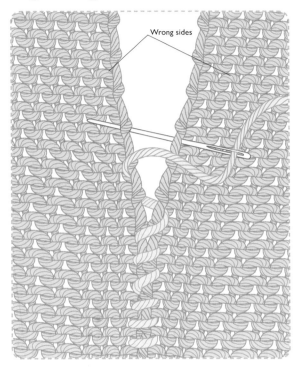

Wrong sides

This seam is suitable for most stitch patterns. Align the pieces of knitting with the WS facing you. Work each stitch of the seam through the little pips formed along the edges of knitting.

Backstitch seam

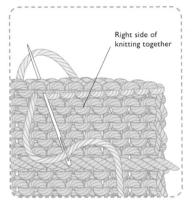

Right side of knitting together

Align the pieces with RS together. Make one stitch forwards, and one stitch back into the starting point of the previous stitch. Work the stitches as close to the edge of the knitting as possible.

Darning in an end

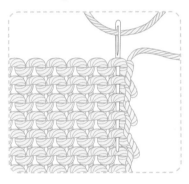

A piece of knitting has at least two yarn ends – at the cast on and cast off edges. For every extra ball of yarn used, there will be two more ends. Thread each end through stitches on the wrong side of your work.

Grafted seam

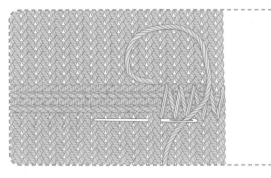

This seam can be worked along two pieces of knitting that have not been cast off or along two cast-off edges as shown here; the principle for both is the same.

1 With the right sides facing you, follow the path of a row of knitting along the seam as shown.

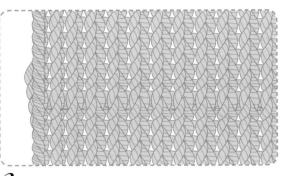

2 When worked in a matching yarn as here, the seam blends in completely and makes it look like a continuous piece of knitting.

fastenings and buttonholes

Choose an appropriate size and material for your project. Although nylon and plastic fastenings are lighter and less obtrusive, metallic or contrast-coloured ones can make a statement. Riveted press studs are useful; insert the shank between stitches and when connecting top to bottom make sure there are no sharp edges.

Attaching press studs

The male side of the stud goes on the inside. Decide position of studs by counting exact stitches and rows on each piece and mark positions with contrast thread.

1 Knot and sew in thread end at marker, catching half of each strand so stitches don't show. Place stud over marker and insert needle near hole just below the stud edge. Bring needle up through stud hole.

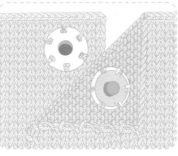

2 Repeat this three or four times through each hole, never taking the needle through to the right side. Move needle to next hole and repeat. To secure thread, sew two small backstitches, then sew a loop, thread the needle back through and pull tightly to secure thread.

Knitted button loop

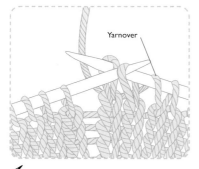

1 Using a cable cast on, cast on as many stitches as required for length of loop. Next row, cast off all stitches.

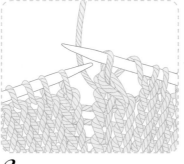

2 Fold the loop in half. Use the ends to sew the loop neatly and firmly to the inside edge of the item.

Open eyelet buttonhole (also used in lace patterns)

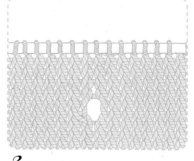

Yarnover

1 For an open eyelet on stocking stitch, work a yarnover on right needle. Work a "sl k1 psso" decrease after yarnover.

2 The yarnover creates a hole and the decrease compensates for the extra loop so the knitting remains the same width.

3 On the following row, purl the yarnover. Open eyelets can be arranged to create any number of lace textures.

Embellishments

Plain knitting sometimes calls out for a little embellishment. Embroidery, pom-poms, or a decorative edging can be the perfect finishing touch and pockets, collars, hems, and cuffs are ideal positions for these.

embroidery on knitting

Bullion stitch and lazy daisies are most commonly used on knitting, although satin stitch can be very attractive and useful for toys, too. Use a smooth yarn that is the same weight as that used for the knitting, or slightly thicker, together with a blunt-ended needle to avoid splitting the knitting yarn.

Bullion stitch

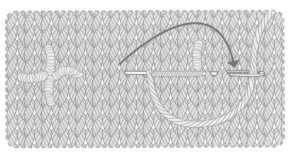

Secure yarn on WS. Bring needle through to RS at one end. Insert needle through to back a short distance from starting point and out again at starting point. Wrap yarn six times around needle and, holding the wraps with your fingers, pull the needle through the wraps. Reinsert the needle through the knitting at the same place (as shown by the arrow). Arrange the bullion stitches in spirals to form roses and stars.

Lazy daisy stitch

Secure yarn on WS and bring needle through at centre of flower. Reinsert needle at starting point and bring it out to front a short distance away. Secure loop with a short stitch. Work all the "petals" in the same way, starting each one at the flower centre.

Satin stitch

1 Secure the yarn on the wrong side. Bring the needle through to front between two stitches, at one side of the shape to be worked.

2 Take the needle to the back between two stitches at the opposite side of the shape.

3 Bring the needle to the front again at the original side, but spacing it a yarn width away by angling the needle very slightly whilst at back of work. The stitches should lie flat and parallel to each other.

4 Continue to work the shape in long stitches that do not pucker the fabric.

swiss darning

Swiss darning imitates and covers the knit stitches on the right side of stocking stitch. It is ideal for small motifs and filling in small intarsia details to save complicated knitting. However, too much can make your work heavy, as you are doubling the yarn on each stitch. Cross stitch books are good sources for small motifs.

Swiss darning worked horizontally

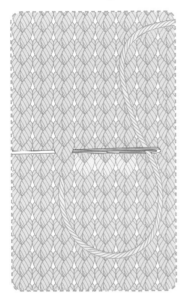

1 Secure the embroidery yarn to the wrong side of the stocking stitch, then pass the needle from back to front through the centre of a knit stitch, and pull the yarn through. Next, insert the needle from right to left behind the knit stitch above as shown and pull the yarn through gently so it "mirrors" the knit stitch size.

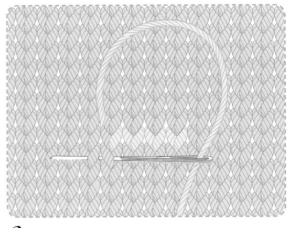

2 Insert the needle from right to left into the knit stitch below and out at the centre of the next knit stitch to the left to complete the stitch as shown. Continue in this way, tracing the path of the knitting horizontally.

Swiss darning worked vertically

1 Secure the embroidery yarn on the wrong side of the stocking stitch, then pass the needle from back to front through the centre of a knit stitch and pull the yarn through. Next, insert the needle from right to left behind the knit stitch above as shown and pull the yarn through.

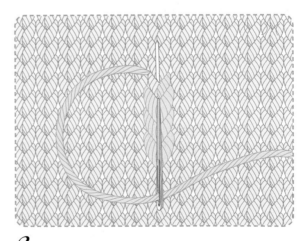

2 Insert the needle from front to back and to front again under the top of the stitch below so it comes out in the centre of the stitch just covered, as shown. Continue in this way, tracing the path of the knitting vertically.

3d embellishments

Surface embellishments and decorations can be attached to knitting once it is completed. These are easy to make and extremely effective, but remember to buy extra yarn. Simple tools are required to make pompoms, whilst a specially worked cast on or cast off edge will make adding a fringe easier.

Fringe

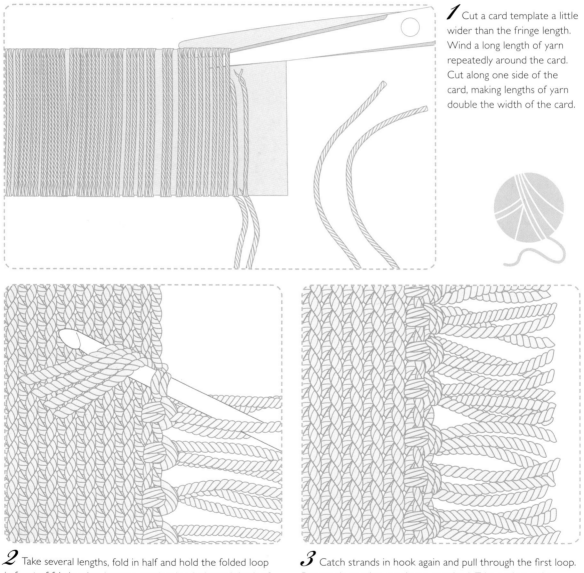

1 Cut a card template a little wider than the fringe length. Wind a long length of yarn repeatedly around the card. Cut along one side of the card, making lengths of yarn double the width of the card.

2 Take several lengths, fold in half and hold the folded loop in front of fabric edge. Insert a crochet hook through back of fabric close to edge or through purpose-made selvedge holes. Catch the folded loop and pull it through to back.

3 Catch strands in hook again and pull through the first loop. Repeat along edge, spacing as required. Trim ends evenly. Fringes can be beaded, knotted, or worked in silky or contrast-coloured yarns.

Pom-poms

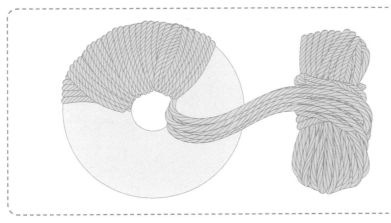

1 Draw two 8cm (3¼in) diameter circles on card. Draw another 2.5cm (1in) diameter circle in the centre. A smaller centre circle makes a denser pom-pom. Cut out circles and centres so they look like doughnuts.

2 Cut several 1m (1yd) lengths of yarn and wind them together into a small ball. Put the circles together. Hold yarn ends at the edge of the circle and insert ball into centre, winding yarn through the circles. Continue winding.

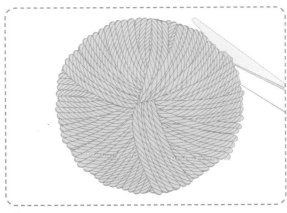

3 If the centre becomes too tight, thread the strands onto a large-eyed needle, and complete the winding. Insert the scissors into the outside of the circle and cut through the wraps.

4 Slide a long, doubled strand of yarn between the circles, wrap and knot it tightly around the core.

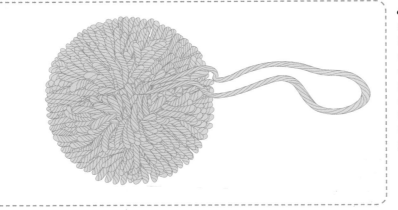

5 Thread the yarn onto a needle and make a few stitches through the knot. Gently remove the circles. Shake and trim the pom-pom, but do not cut the tie strands. Suspending a wool pom-pom in steam will make it fuller (hang it at the end of a long needle for safety). Your pattern may call for a pom-pom in another size, just adjust your circle sizes accordingly.

Glossary

aran yarn Also called medium, 12-ply, worsted, or Afghan (yarn symbol 4). A medium yarn suitable for jumpers, blankets, hats, scarves, and mittens.

backstitch A sewing stitch used for firm, straight seam, which is worked from the wrong side.

ballband The wrapper around a ball of yarn, which usually details fibre content, weight, length, needle size, tension, and cleaning instructions.

bias knitting Diagonally shaped pieces of knitting, which slope to the left of right.

blocking The finishing process for a piece of knitting, in which it is set in shape using water or steam.

bulky or chunky yarn Also called 14-ply, craft, or rug (yarn symbol 5). A chunky yarn is suitable for rugs, jackets, blankets, hats, leg-warmers, and winter accessories.

cable A design made by crossing one or more stitches over other stitches in a row; frequently resembles a rope of cable. Twist stitches belong to the same family.

cable cast on A method of casting on that produces a firm, cord-like edge, which holds a neat and defined edge.

carrying up the side A method for keeping the edges of a two-coloured, even-row stripe pattern tidy. The yarns are twisted around each other and carried up the side of the piece.

cast off in pattern Cast off while working stitches in the pattern used in the previous row.

cast off in ribbing Cast off while working stitches in the ribbing used in the previous row.

casting off/binding off Completing a piece of knitting by finishing off the loops of the stitches so that they cannot unravel.

casting off knitwise/purlwise Cast off while working the stitches is knit/purl.

casting on Forming an initial number of stitches on a needle at the start of a piece of knitting. There are various methods, depending on the effect you want to achieve.

circular knitting Working on circular needles of double-pointed needles to produce a seamless item such as a hat. There is no need to turn the work and no wrong-side row. Sometimes called tubular knitting.

circular needles A pair of needles connected by a flexible tube, usually used for circular knitting and very wide projects that do not fit on conventional straight needles.

colourwork Any method of incorporating colour into you knitting. This includes stripes, Fair Isle, intarsia, and slipped stitch patterns.

darning in ends The process of completing a piece of knitting by weaving yarn ends (such as from the cast on and cast off edges) into the knitting to disguise them.

decreases/decreasing Techniques that subtract stitches. Used to shape knitting and to form textures in combination with other stitches.

double-knit yarn (DK) A medium-weight yarn. Also called 5–6-ply, or light worsted (yarn symbol 3). A light yarn suitable for jumpers, lightweight scarves, blankets and toys.

double-pointed needles Knitting needles with a tip at each end; a set of four or five is used for the circular knitting of small items, such as mittens and socks.

Fair Isle A method in which yarn colours not being worked are carried across the back of the work until required. This unworked yarn can also be woven in.

fibres Yarn is made up of fibres, such as the hair from an animal, man-made (synthetic) fibres, or fibres derived from a plant. The fibres are processed and spun into yarn.

fine yarn Also called 4-ply, sport, or baby (yarn symbol 2). A fine yarn suitable for lightweight jumpers, babywear, socks, and accessories.

fully fashioned shaping An attractive method for increasing and decreasing when working stocking stitch, in which a line of stitches is preserved to follow the edge of the piece.

garter stitch Working in knit stitches on every row, whichever side of the knitting is facing you. It produces a thick fabric, which is identical on both sides and will not curl at the edges.

i-cord A narrow tube of knitting, created on a knitting dolly or cord-maker, or knitted on double-pointed needles. Used as cords, straps, ties, or as a trimming.

increases/increasing Created stitches during knitting. Can be combined with other stitches in order to form shapes and textures.

intarsia A method for working with different coloured yarns to create blocks of colour. A separate length of yarn is used for each colour of the motif and twisted where the colour changes to prevent holes; yarns are not stranded across the reverse of the work. Uses less yarn than Fair Isle knitting.

knit stitch One of two basic stitches used to form knitting.

knit-on cast on This cast on uses two needles to combine a cast on with the knitting of the first row. If worked through the front of the loops, it produces a soft edge; if through the back of the loops, the edge is firmer.

knitting through back of loop Stitches that twist the stitch in the row below so that the legs of the stitch cross at the base.

knitwise Working with knit stitches facing you, insert the right-hand needle into a stitch as if to knit it.

lace yarn Also called 2-ply or fingering (yarn symbol 0). A very fine yarn for knitting lace.

live stitches Stitches that are currently being worked.

mattress stitch A seaming stitch, which is almost invisible, used to sew pieces of knitting together with the right sides facing. It only forms a small seam on the wrong side of the work.

mercerized cotton Cotton thread, fabric, or yarn that has been treated in order to strengthen it and add sheen. The yarn is a good choice for items that need to be strong and hold a shape.

organic wool Wool produced from sheep that graze on land that is not treated with herbicides, pesticides, or artificial fertilizers. The wool is not given any man-made chemical treatments.

oversewing/overcasting Stitch used to seam two pieces of knitting by placing them right sides together and then sewing through the edge stitches. Also called whip stitch.

pick up and knit Draw loops through the edge of the knitting and place them on the needle.

pilling When the surface of a knitted item rubs up into tiny balls, due to wear and friction.

plied yarn A yarn made from more than one strand of spun fibre, so 4-ply yarn is four strands plied together. Most knitting yarns are plied, as plying prevents the yarn twisting and resulting fabric slanting diagonally.

pom-pom A small, fluffy ball made of yarn, used as trimming or decoration.

purl stitch One of two basic stitches used to form knitting.

purlwise Working stitches facing you, inserting the right-hand needle into a stitch as if to purl it.

ribbing/rib/rib stitch Knitting with great elasticity, used where fabric needs to hold tightly to the body, but is capable of expanding. Single ribbing or 1×1 rib is knit 1, purl 1; 2×2 rib is knit 2, purl 2; 3×3 rib is knit 3, purl 3.

short-row shaping Used for shaping shoulders, curving hems, making darts, and tuning sock heels. Rows are added in only one part of the fabric by knitting part of a row instead of knitting it to the end. It uses one of three turning methods to close holes.

slip knot A knot that you form when you place the first loop on the needle as you start casting on stitches.

slip stitch Sliding a stitch from the left-hand needle to the right-hand needle without working it. The usual method is to slip the stitches purlwise; less frequently, stitches are slipped knitwise. Slipped stitches at the beginning of each row – slipped selvedges – can help to create a very neat edge.

stocking stitch A stitch formed by knitting all stitches when the right side of the work is facing you, and purling all stitches when the wrong side of the work is facing you.

super bulky or super chunky yarn Also called 16-ply (and upwards), bulky yarn, or roving (yarn symbol 6). A chunky yarn suitable for heavy blankets, rugs, and thick scarves.

superfine yarn Also called 3-ply, fingering or baby (yarn symbol 1). A very fine yarn suitable for fine-knit socks, shawls, and babywear.

tension The size of the stitches in a piece of knitting (US: gauge), measured by the number of stitches and rows to 10cm (4in), or to 2.5cm (1in) on fine knitting.

tension square A square knitted to the required number of stitches and rows to match the stated tension of a project, usually 10cm (4in) square. A knitter must achieve the tension stated in a pattern, or else the knitted item will not end up the correct size.

three-needle cast off/bind-off A method of casting off which binds two sets of stitches together, whilst casting off simultaneously. This creates a firm, neat seam, with a smooth finish on the rights side of the work. It is a good way of finishing the toe of a sock or the fingertip area of a mitten.

twist Two stitches twisted together to form a narrow cable, which slants left or right. A cable needle is not used.

work straight Work in the specified pattern without increasing or decreasing (US: work even).

yarn Fibres that have been spun into a long strand in order for you to knit with them. Yarns may be made of natural fibres, a blend of two, or even non-standard materials.

yarn bobbins Small plastic shapes for holding yarn when doing intarsia work, where there are many yarns in different colours.

yarnover (yo) An instruction to increase by adding stitches and creating holes at the same time. Yarnovers (yo) are used for decorative purposes, such as producing lacy knitting. There are various types : yfwd (US: yo), yarnover between knit stitches; yrn (US: yo), yarnover between purl stitches; yfrn and yon (US: yo), yarnover between knit and purl stitches; and yfwd (US: yo), yarnover at the beginning of a row.

Index

Acknowledgments

Dorling Kindersley would like to thank the following people for their hard work and contributions towards *Baby and Toddler Knits Made Easy*:

Knitting designers Caroline Birkett, Debi Birkin, Sian Brown, Lara Evans, Fiona Goble, Zoe Halstead, Susie Johns, Val Pierce, and Woolly Wormhead

Knitters Brenda Bostock, June Cole, Antonella Conti, Sally Cuthbert, Joan Doyle, Eva Hallas, Dolly Howes, Brenda Jennings, Maisie Lawrence, Patricia Liddle, Ann McFaull, Karen Tattersall, Jane Wales, and Brenda Willows

Pattern checkers Carol Ibbetson and Rachel Vowles

Proofreader Angela Baynham

Indexer Marie Lorimer

Design assistance Charlotte Johnson, Nicola Rodway, and Clare Patane

Editorial assistance Katharine Goddard and Grace Redhead

Additional photography Dave King

Photography assistant Julie Stewart

Props George & Beth and Backgrounds

Location for photography 1st Option

The following yarn manufacturers and distributors for supplying yarn for the projects Coats Crafts UK, King Cole Ltd, Sirdar Yarns, and Sublime Yarns

Models Celia Arn, George Grapnell, Rosie Grapnell, Dexter Kelly, Eirinn Kelly, Stella Kelly, Henry Michael Kershaw, Jessica Catherine Kershaw, Ellode Lyons, Emily MacKrill, Thomas MacKrill, Ryan O'Kane, Blake Reeder, Harrison Singer Naseworthy, Alfie Skelton, Abigail van Rooijen, and Matilde van Rooijen

About the consultant

Dr Vikki Haffenden has an active career in all aspects of hand and machine knitting and knitwear design. She is the co-author of Dorling Kindersley's *The Knitting Book* and the consultant on *Knit Step-by-Step*. Her particular interest is the exploration of technical knitting for the design development of knitted textiles and garment shapes. Vikki holds a PhD based in commercial knitting and knitwear design research, and currently teaches in the department of Knitted Textiles at the University of Brighton in Sussex.

Happy knitting!